Tragedy / *Clifford Leech*

Routledge
LONDON and NEW YORK

First published 1969
by Methuen & Co. Ltd
Reprinted six times

Reprinted 1989 by
Routledge
11 New Fetter Lane, London EC4P 4EE
29 West 35th Street, New York, NY 10001

© 1969 Clifford Leech

Printed in Great Britain
by J. W. Arrowsmith Ltd, Bristol

ISBN 0-415-04599-1

Contents

FOUNDER EDITOR'S PREFACE	*page* viii
PREFATORY NOTE	ix
1 Some Definitions and Observations	1
2 Tragedy in Practice and in Theory	12
3 The Tragic Hero	33
4 Cleansing? or Sacrifice?	47
5 The Sense of Balance	56
6 Peripeteia, Anagnorisis, Suffering	61
7 The Chorus and the Unities	70
8 The Sense of Overdoing It	77
SELECT BIBLIOGRAPHY	82
INDEX	87

Founder Editor's Preface

The volumes composing the Critical Idiom deal with a wide variety of key terms in our critical vocabulary. The purpose of the series differs from that served by the standard glossaries of literary terms. Many terms are adequately defined for the needs of students by the brief entries in these glossaries, and such terms do not call for attention in the present series. But there are other terms which cannot be made familiar by means of compact definitions. Students need to grow accustomed to them through simple and straightforward but reasonably full discussions. The main purpose of this series is to provide such discussions.

Many critics have borrowed methods and criteria from currently influential bodies of knowledge or belief that have developed without particular reference to literature. In our own century, some of them have drawn on art-history, psychology, or sociology. Others, strong in a comprehensive faith, have looked at literature and literary criticism from a Marxist or a Christian or some other sharply defined point of view. The result has been the importation into literary criticism of terms from the vocabularies of these sciences and creeds. Discussions of such bodies of knowledge and belief in their bearing upon literature and literary criticism form a natural extension of the initial aim of the Critical Idiom.

Because of their diversity of subject-matter, the studies in the series vary considerably in structure. But all authors have tried to give as full illustrative quotation as possible, to make reference whenever appropriate to more than one literature, and to write in such a way as to guide readers towards the short bibliographies in which they have made suggestions for further reading.

John D. Jump

University of Manchester

Prefatory Note

It has, I feel, been a great privilege to be asked by Professor John Jump to write the volume on 'Tragedy' for this series, yet of course few tasks could have been more difficult. A volume of a hundred thousand words, though it might have taken longer, would have been in some respects easier. What is here presented is a cursory glance at what 'tragedy' has meant through the ages, yet I hope that the term may have been in this way somewhat clarified.

Dates of plays are those of first performance (preceded by a '*c.*' where the date is uncertain), unless otherwise indicated. Quotations from Shakespeare are from the edition by Peter Alexander (1951); act-, scene-, and line-divisions are from the Globe edition.

In the text, as in the bibliography, the place of publication is London unless otherwise indicated.

I am grateful to Messrs. Hamish Hamilton Ltd and Alfred A. Knopf for permission to include the quotation from Jean-Paul Sartre's *Les Mouches*, translated by Stuart Gilbert, on pp. 51–2 and to Hope Leresche and Steel and Jonathan Cape Ltd for permission to include the quotation from *Tango* by Slawomir Mrozek, translated by N. Bethell, on p. 11.

Clifford Leech

Toronto, 1969

I

Some Definitions and Observations

ARISTOTLE

A tragedy, then, is the imitation of an action that is serious and also, as having magnitude, complete in itself; in language with pleasurable accessories, each kind brought in separately in the parts of the work; in a dramatic, not in a narrative form; with incidents arousing pity and fear, wherewith to accomplish its catharsis of such emotions.

(*The Poetics*, Oxford, 1909, translated by Ingram Bywater, Chapter VI)

Plots are either simple or complex, since the actions they represent are naturally of this twofold description. The action, proceeding in the way defined, as one continuous whole, I call simple, when the change in the hero's fortunes takes place without Peripety or Discovery; and complex, when it involves one or the other, or both. These should each of them arise out of the structure of the Plot itself, so as to be the consequence, necessary or probable, of the antecedents. There is a great difference between a thing happening *propter hoc* and *post hoc*.

(*The Poetics*, Chapter X)

There remains, then, the intermediate kind of personage, a man not pre-eminently virtuous and just, whose misfortune, however, is brought upon him not by vice and depravity but by some error of judgement, of the number of those in the enjoyment of great reputation and prosperity; e.g. Oedipus, Thyestes, and the men of note of similar families. The perfect Plot, accordingly, must have a single, and not (as some tell us) a double issue; the change in the hero's fortunes must be not from misery to happiness, but on the contrary from happiness to misery; and the cause of it must lie not in any depravity, but in some great error on his part; the man himself being either such as we have described, or better, not worse, than that.

(*The Poetics*, Chapter XIII)

DIOMEDES (4th century A.D.)

[Tragedy is] a narrative of the fortunes of heroic (or semi-divine) characters in adversity.

(J. W. H. Atkins, *English Literary Criticism: The Medieval Phase*, Cambridge, 1943, p. 31)

ISIDORE OF SEVILLE (6th–7th centuries A.D.)

[Tragedy consists of] sad stories of commonwealths and kings.

(Atkins, p. 32)

JOHN OF GARLAND (12th – 13th centuries A.D.)

[Tragedy is] a poem written in the 'grand' style, which treats of shameful and wicked deeds, and, beginning in joy, ends in grief.

(Atkins, p. 111)

CHAUCER

Tragedie is to seyn a certeyn storie,
As olde bokes maken us memorie,
Of him that stood in greet prosperitee
And is y-fallen out of heigh degree
Into miserie, and endeth wrecchedly.

(Prologue to *The Monk's Tale*)

SIDNEY

... the high and excellent Tragedy, that openeth the greatest wounds, and showeth forth the ulcers that are covered with tissue; that maketh kings fear to be tyrants, and tyrants manifest their tyrannical humours; that, with stirring the affects of admiration and commiseration, teacheth the uncertainty of this world, and upon how weak foundations gilden roofs are builded ...

> (*An Apology for Poetry, English Critical Essays (Sixteenth, Seventeenth and Eighteenth Centuries)*, edited by Edmund D. Jones, 1930, pp. 31–2)

GEORGE PUTTENHAM

Besides those Poets *Comick* there were other who serued also the stage, but medled not with so base matters: For they set forth the dolefull falls of infortunate & afflicted Princes, & were called Poets *Tragicall*.

> (*The Arte of English Poesie* (1589), edited by G. D. Willcock and A. Walker, Cambridge, 1936, p. 26)

ANON

> Murder be proud, and Tragedy laugh on,
> I'll seek a stage for thee to jet upon.

> > (*Lust's Dominion, or The Lascivious Queen*, probably acted 1599–1600)

JOHN MARSTON

> If any spirit breathes within this round,
> Uncapable of waightie passion
> (As from his birth, being hugged in the armes,
> And nuzzled twixt the breastes of happinesse)
> Who winkes, and shuts his apprehension up
> From common sense of what men were, and are,
> Who would not knowe what men must be; let such
> Hurrie amaine from our black visag'd showes:

We shall affright their eyes. But if a breast,
Nail'd to the earth with griefe: if any heart
Pierc't through with anguish, pant within this ring:
If there be any blood, whose heate is choakt
And stifled with true sense of misery:
If ought of these straines fill this consort up,
Th' arrive most welcome.

(Prologue to *Antonio's Revenge,*
c. 1600)

SHAKESPEARE

Whereupon it [Reason] made this threne
To the phoenix and the dove,
Co-supremes and stars of love,
As chorus to their tragic scene.

(*The Phoenix and Turtle,* 1601)

CHAPMAN

And for the authentical truth of either person or action, who (worth
the respecting) will expect it in a poem, whose subject is not truth,
but things like truth? Poor envious souls they are that cavil at truth's
want in these natural fictions; material instruction, elegant and sen-
tentious excitation to virtue, and deflection from her contrary, being
the soul, limbs, and limits of an authentical tragedy.

(Dedication to *The Revenge of Bussy
D'Ambois,* published 1613)

 RACINE

Ce n'est point une nécessité qu'il y ait du sang et des morts dans une
tragédie; il suffit que l'action en soit grande, que les acteurs en soient
héroïques, que les passions y soient excitées, et que tout s'y ressente
de cette tristesse majestueuse qui fait tout le plaisir de la tragédie.
[It is not necessary that there shall be blood and deaths in tragedy:

it is enough that its action shall be great, that its characters shall be heroic, that the passions shall be aroused through it, and that the whole effect shall be that majestic sadness which constitutes the whole pleasure of tragedy.]

(Preface to *Bérénice*, 1668)

THOMAS RYMER

These [the Greek writers of tragedy] were for teaching by *examples*, in a graver way, yet extremely *pleasant* and *delightful*. And, finding in History, the same *end* happen to the *righteous* and to the *unjust*, *vertue* often opprest, and *wickedness* on the Throne: they saw these particular *yesterday-truths* were imperfect and unproper to illustrate the *universal* and *eternal truths* by them intended. Finding also that this *unequal* distribution of rewards and punishments did perplex the *wisest*, and by the *Atheist* was made a scandal to the *Divine Providence*. They concluded, that a *Poet* must of necessity see *justice* exactly administerd, if he intended to please. For, said they, if the World can scarce be satisfi'd with God Almighty, whose holy will and purposes are not to be *comprehended*; a *Poet* (in these matters) shall never be pardon'd, who (they are sure) is not *incomprehensible*; whose *ways* and *walks* may, without *impiety*, be penetrated and examin'd.

(*The Tragedies of the Last Age*, 1677)

DRYDEN

The death of *Anthony* and *Cleopatra*, is a Subject which has been treated by the greatest Wits of our Nation, after *Shakespeare*; and by all so variously, that their Example has given me the confidence to try my selfe in this Bowe of *Ulysses* amongst the Crowd of Sutors; and, withal, to take my own measures, in aiming at the Mark. I doubt not but the same Motive has prevailed with all of us in this attempt; I mean the excellency of the Moral: for the chief Persons represented, were famous Patterns of unlawful Love; and their end accordingly was unfortunate.

(Preface to *All for Love*, published 1678)

ADDISON

The English writers of tragedy are possessed with a notion, that when they represent a virtuous or innocent person in distress, they ought not to leave him till they have delivered him out of his troubles, or made him triumph over his enemies. This error they have been led into by a ridiculous doctrine in modern criticism, that they are obliged to an equal distribution of rewards and punishments, and an impartial execution of poetical justice. Who were the first that established this rule I know not; but I am sure it has no foundation in nature, in reason, or in the practice of the ancients.

(*The Spectator*, 16 April 1711)

HEINRICH VON KLEIST

> Man can be great in grief, ay, even a hero,
> But only in happiness is he a god.

(*Penthesilea*, 1808, translated by Humphrey Trevelyan)

GOETHE

Even a noble Greek who well knew how to portray heroic characters did not disdain to let his heroes weep when they suffered such agony. He said: Noble are the men who can weep. Leave me alone – you who have a dry heart and dry eyes! I curse the happy for whom the unhappy is only a spectacle.

(*Elective Affinities*, 1809, translated by E. Mayer and L. Bogan)

KIERKEGAARD

The tragic hero does not know the terrible responsibility of solitude. In the next place he has the comfort that he can weep and lament with Clytemnestra and Iphigenia – and tears and cries are assuaging, but unutterable sighs are torture.

(*Fear and Trembling*, 1843, translated by Walter Lowrie, New York, 1953, p. 123)

NIETZSCHE

... tragic myth has convinced us that even the ugly and discordant are merely an esthetic game which the will, in its utter exuberance, plays with itself. In order to understand the difficult phenomenon of Dionysiac art directly, we must now attend to the supreme significance of *musical dissonance*. The delight created by tragic myth has the same origin as the delight dissonance in music creates. That primal Dionysiac delight, experienced even in the presence of pain, is the source common to both music and tragic myth.

(*The Birth of Tragedy*, 1872, translated by Francis Golffing, New York, 1956, p. 143)

HENRY JAMES

She was older for him to-night, visibly less exempt from the touch of time; but she was as much as ever the finest and subtlest creature, the happiest apparition, it had been given him, in all his years, to meet; and yet he could see her there as vulgarly troubled, in very truth, as a maidservant crying for her young man. The only thing was that she judged herself as the maidservant wouldn't; the weakness of which wisdom too, the dishonour of which judgement, seemed but to sink her lower. Her collapse, however, no doubt, was briefer and she had in a manner recovered herself before he intervened. 'Of course I'm afraid for my life. But that's nothing. It isn't that.'

(*The Ambassadors*, 1903, Book XII, §II)

A. C. BRADLEY

Thus we are left at last with an idea showing two sides or aspects which we can neither separate nor reconcile. The whole or order against which the individual part shows itself powerless seems to be animated by a passion for perfection: we cannot otherwise explain its behaviour towards evil. Yet it appears to engender this evil within itself, and in its effort to overcome and expel it it is agonised with pain, and driven to mutilate its own substance and to lose not only evil but priceless good. That this idea, though very different from the idea of a blank fate, is no solution of the riddle of life is obvious; but why should we expect it to be such a solution? Shakespeare was not attempting to justify the way of God to men, or to show the universe as a Divine Comedy. He was writing tragedy, and tragedy would not be tragedy if it were not a painful mystery.

> (*Shakespearean Tragedy*, 1904, pp. 37–8)

I. A. RICHARDS

Tragedy is only possible to a mind which is for the moment agnostic or Manichean. The least touch of any theology which has a compensating Heaven to offer the tragic hero is fatal. . . . Tragedy is perhaps the most general, all-accepting, all-ordering experience known. It can take anything into its organisation, modifying it so that it finds a place. It is invulnerable; there is nothing which does not present to the tragic attitude *when fully developed* a fitting aspect and only a fitting aspect.

> (*Principles of Literary Criticism*, reprinted 1934, pp. 246–7)

JEAN ANOUILH

The spring is wound up tight. It will uncoil of itself. That is what is so convenient in tragedy. The least little turn of the wrist will do the job. . . .
The rest is automatic. You don't need to lift a finger. The machine is in perfect order; it has been oiled ever since time began, and it runs without friction. Death, treason and sorrow are on the march; and they move in the wake of storm, of tears, of stillness. Every kind of stillness. The hush when the executioner's axe goes up at the end of the last act. The unbreathable silence when, at the beginning of the play, the two lovers, their hearts bared, their bodies naked, stand for

the first time face to face in the darkened room, afraid to stir. . . .
Tragedy is clean, it is restful, it is flawless. It has nothing to do with
melodrama – with wicked villains, persecuted maidens, avengers,
sudden revelations and eleventh-hour repentances. Death, in a melodrama, is really horrible because it is never inevitable. . . .

In a tragedy, nothing is in doubt and everyone's destiny is known.
That makes for tranquillity. There is a sort of fellow-feeling among
characters in a tragedy: he who kills is as innocent as he who gets
killed: it's all a matter of what part you are playing. Tragedy is restful; and the reason is that hope, that foul, deceitful thing, has no part
in it. There isn't any hope. You're trapped. The whole sky has fallen
on you, and all you can do about it is to shout.

Don't mistake me: I said 'shout': I did not say groan, whimper,
complain. That, you cannot do. But you can shout aloud; you can get
all those things said that you never thought you'd be able to say – or
never even knew you had it in you to say. And you don't say these
things because it will do any good to say them: you know better than
that. You say them for their own sake; you say them because you
learn a lot from them.

> (*Antigone*, 1942, translated by Lewis
> Galantière, 1951)

GEORGE STEINER

But one cannot conclude from Claudel's bizarre and private genius
that the Christian world view is about to produce a body of tragic
drama. Claudel was less a Christian than a special and somewhat
terrifying kind of Roman Catholic. He was of the age of Gregory
rather than of the modern church. The glow of hell-fire seemed to
evoke in him a stern approval, nearly a delight in the vengeful grandeur of God's ways. There are pages in his dramas and scriptural
commentaries which read as if they had been discovered in a monastic
library and were the labour of some tyrannic abbot looking out upon
the corruptions of man.

> (*The Death of Tragedy*, 1961, pp.
> 340–1)

JOHN HOPKINS

> *Mother.* How could you say – how – Alan – could you want me to be dead? [*Silence.*]
>
> *Alan.* Nothing particularly special about that. I want everyone to be dead – one time or another. It's my favourite solution. If only – he, she or it – was dead. [ALAN *walks away, round the table, leaving his* MOTHER.] The tragedy – concern – the bravery in time of trouble. The spot-light and the centre stage. Deep inside – relief – 'cause all the problems, all the bitterness – and beastliness – hard words and hatred – gone away.

> (*Talking to a Stranger*, 1967, p. 323)

BERTRAND RUSSELL

> One of the things that make literature so consoling is that its tragedies are all in the past, and have the completeness and repose that comes of being beyond the reach of our endeavours. It is a most wholesome thing, when one's sorrow grows acute, to view it as having all happened long, long ago: to join, in imagination, the mournful company of dim souls whose lives were sacrificed to the great machine that still grinds on. I see the past, like a sunny landscape, where the world's mourners mourn no longer. On the banks of the river of Time, the sad procession of human generations is marching slowly to the grave; but in the quiet country of the past, the tired wanderers rest, and all their weeping is stilled.

> (*The Autobiography of Bertrand Russell 1872–1914*, 1967, p. 169)

TOM STOPPARD

> Wheels have been set in motion, and they have their own pace, to which we are . . . condemned. Each move is dictated by the previous one – that is the meaning of order. If we start being arbitrary it'll just be a shambles: at least, let us hope so. Because if we happened, just happened to discover, or even suspect, that our spontaneity was part of their order, we'd know that we were lost.

> (*Rosencrantz and Guildenstern are Dead* (1966), 1967, pp. 42–3)

SLAWOMIR MROZEK

Stomil. . . . Now let's talk sense. You want to bring the world back to normal – don't ask me why, that's your business and I've had my fill of it. I have never interfered before but this time you've gone too far. Oh yes – what a splendid idea! – a tragic resolution – that's just what you needed. Up to now tragedy has always been the final throw of societies based on rigid ideas. So you thought you'd push me into a tragic act. That would save a lot of messing about, wouldn't it? – no need for laborious reconstruction – you'd have got it made. And if someone happens to die in the process, or your father goes to gaol, if not worse, that's of no concern as long as you gain your end. A tragedy would suit you fine, wouldn't it? You know what you are? – you're just a dirty little formalist. You don't give a damn about me, or your mother. They can all drop dead so long as the form is preserved. And worst of all you don't even care about yourself. You're a fanatic! . . .

Stomil. So what do you get out of sacrificing me?

Arthur. Something would be achieved. Tragically, it's true. You're right there, Father, and I'm sorry. Nevertheless, tragedy is a great and powerful convention, reality would be trapped within it.

Stomil. You fool – is that what you think? Don't you see that nowadays tragedy isn't possible any more? Reality is stronger than any convention, even tragedy. Do you know what you'd have got if I'd shot him?

Arthur. Something irrevocable, something on the scale of the old masters.

Stomil. Not at all. A farce, that's what. Today farce is the only thing possible. A corpse is no help at all. Why not accept this? – Farce can still be fine art.

> (*Tango*, translated by N. Bethell, adapted by T. Stoppard, 1968, pp. 62–3, 64)

2

Tragedy in Practice and in Theory

For Europe – and Europe alone provided tragedy as we know it, until it lent its findings to the rest of the world – tragedy began in Greece, and our first records are from the fifth century B.C. As Allardyce Nicoll (*World Drama*, 1949, pp. 25–6) has pointed out, Egypt may have provided an example in the second or third millennium B.C., but the earliest texts are from Athens. We have evidence enough that the form arose from a choral song in honour of Dionysus, that this became first an alternation between a single actor's speech and the chorus, and then (in Aeschylus) a use of either monologue (as prominently in the *Agamemnon*) or duologue in alternation with the chorus; in Sophocles and Euripides there could be three actors simultaneously used, with the chorus occupying a smaller but still important part.

But what was the chorus saying, what were the actors implying through their masked speech? They told of man's subjection to the gods, of the ineluctable result of the evil act (whether willed, as in Agamemnon's sacrifice of his daughter Iphigenia, or un-willed, as in Oedipus' killing of his father and marriage with his mother), of the fact that through suffering men had the oppor-tunity of growing. Oedipus is seen as holy in Colonus, not despite but because of his guilt accompanied by his full recognition of it. These dramatists offered no promise of an after-life of bliss for the man who won to such recognition: the thing was good in itself. It was good for a man to know what man is, how guilty he is. There was a kind of 'redemption' in the act of recognition itself. The

Greek idea was essentially cognitive: let man know, for good or ill. In Euripides' *Iphigenia in Tauris*, Orestes is saved from death when Iphigenia knows who he is. But in some circumstances there can be no saving from death: Antigone in Sophocles' play must die because she has seen it is her duty to perform the burial rites for her slain brother. In the same play Creon realizes how much he has to suffer, with the loss of his son, because he has refused to recognize the categorical imperative that Antigone faces. On the other hand, the *Oresteia* of Aeschylus ends in peace, with Orestes granted pardon through the casting-vote of Athene when he is brought before the court of the Areopagus to answer the charge of matricide, and in the *Prometheia* (of which only the first part, the *Prometheus Bound*, has survived) it appears that ultimately Zeus and Prometheus were reconciled – the great god and the great rebel – so that a place was found in the total scheme of things for both. For the Greeks, tragedy was a rite in honour of the presiding god Dionysus, whose priests were present in reserved seats, like canons in a cathedral. It did not have to end badly, and several of our extant plays, including some of Euripides, seem in our sense to belong to comedy rather than to tragedy: the *Ion* has been adapted into a generally comic form in T. S. Eliot's *The Confidential Clerk*, and the *Helen* and the *Alcestis* (also giving Eliot his cue, for *The Cocktail Party*) do not seem 'tragic' to us.

Moreover, the Greek dramatists were accustomed to the idea of a trilogy of tragic plays followed by a satyr-play (a grotesque, semi-romantic affair involving gods and heroes, comparable almost to the harlequinade in a nineteenth-century English pantomime). The trilogy became gradually looser in concept. The only complete one we have is Aeschylus' *Oresteia*, but even Euripides' *The Trojan Women* is the third of three plays on the Trojan War, offered together on a single occasion. What is everywhere evident is that, for the Greek dramatists of the fifth century B.C., the idea of 'tragedy' was a vague one: it presented terrible things about great people; it might offer a final consolation (as in the *Oresteia* and the *Prometheia*); it might draw back from reconciliation, as *The Trojan Women*, the third part of a trilogy, undoubtedly did; it might end in only an ironic conclusion. And always afterwards there was the satyr-play, shrugging away any sense of the terrible but making its own mock of gods and heroes.

For long after the fifth century there must have been many plays written in Hellas, and of course the plays of the three great masters – Aeschylus, Sophocles, Euripides – continued to be acted. But we know little of the work that followed the great period. We have an imaginative reconstruction of how the old plays were acted throughout Hellas in the next century in Mary Renault's novel *The Mask of Apollo* (1966). At that time separate plays, divorced from the trilogies to which they originally belonged, may well have been acted and have thus exhibited without qualification the special anguish of the heroes. And in the fourth century, too, Aristotle wrote *The Poetics*, probably preserved for us only through the lecture-notes of a disciple and limited mainly to tragic writing. Aristotle was not generally prescriptive: he wanted primarily, as he did throughout the world of nature, to describe what he found. But he deduced from the tragedies he had seen and read that there were certain general characteristics of the tragic hero, of the effect of tragedy, of the time-span of a single tragedy, and also of the structural devices commonly used in tragic writing. So he argued that, for tragedy as for all arts, we have *mimesis*, an 'imitation' of what is in the world about us, and, peculiar to tragedy, an effect of *catharsis*. What he says about *catharsis* constitutes one of the most disputed matters in relation to the Kind, and we shall have to return to it. His principal comment on the nature of the tragic hero has been quoted in Chapter 1, and this also is not necessarily to be accepted. But his emphasis on *peripeteia* and *anagnorisis* (particularly the latter) are, we shall see, of major importance throughout the history of tragic writing.

Latin tragedy in the theatres existed, but we know almost nothing about it. Seneca's plays, so influential in the Renaissance, were written in Nero's time and, it appears certain, were recited by a single speaker before a small audience which knew how dangerous was the situation in which they were living. It is not surprising that the imagery and the subject-matter of these plays is violent, hell-ridden: no one hearing them knew where the Emperor's next blow would fall, and all who heard them, being patricians, were especially vulnerable. Seneca depended on the Greeks for his material. He could find refuge from his particular situation only in stoicism, contrasting the violence of his plays' actions with a rejection, in his chorus-speeches, of the world of high place. These tragedies probably achieved their first theatrical performances in sixteenth-century Italy.

In the Middle Ages the term 'tragedy' lost all connection with the idea of performance. The quotations from Diomedes, Isidore of Seville, and Chaucer in Chapter 1 show that it had become simply descriptive of the pattern of a narrative. Only gradually in the centuries following the fall of Rome did the drama come back to Europe – first in the form of presenting parts of the Christian interpretation of world-history, and then as a vehicle for a moral lesson, in an allegorical form, which would help the individual soul to salvation. Of course, there were 'tragic moments' in such writing – that is, moments when the audience might feel the dreadfulness of things – but these were subsumed within a total system which affirmed God's promises, God's plan. For the Middle Ages, 'tragedy' was simply a story which ended unhappily, offering a warning that, if one were not careful, a final unhappiness would be one's own lot too. It told, we have seen in the quotations in Chapter 1, of great people and public events, so it was dignified: the implication was that the common man's damnation was not its concern. And then in the Renaissance men wanted to imitate the dreadfulness and authority of Seneca. It was not altogether easy to do so, for his heroes were remote and their fates belonged to a pre-Christian mode of thinking. When Thomas Sackville and Thomas Norton wrote *Gorboduc*, which used to be called 'the first English tragedy', in 1561, it was much more a 'political morality' – that is, a didactic play on the need to govern a kingdom properly – than a tragedy, which implies surely, for us in the last two centuries, an exposition of man's powerlessness in his cosmic setting. Yet the authors were obviously wanting to write 'tragedy' and were praised by Sidney in his *Apology for Poetry* for 'climbing to the height of Seneca's style'. It should be noted how rare is the word 'tragedy' on title-pages in the late Elizabethan and Jacobean years that followed. Marlowe, whom we customarily think of as the first major tragic writer of the Elizabethan-Jacobean years, had his *Tamburlaine* published in 1590 as 'Deuided into two Tragicall Discourses' (which is indeed vague), and his *Doctor Faustus* appeared as a 'Tragicall History' in 1604. Shakespeare's *King Lear* was published as a 'True Chronicle Historie' in 1608. The 1623 Shakespeare Folio was divided into three sections (comedies, histories, tragedies), but even there some uncertainty appeared: *Cymbeline* was included among the tragedies, and *Troilus and Cressida* was originally meant to be there. We have seen in Chapter 1 that Sidney saw 'admiration' and warning as implicit in tragic writing, though the very idea of warning seems to run counter to our modern conception of tragedy (as well as to Greek tragedy) and 'admiration' too is suspect. We may wonder whether we dare to offer admiration when we are in the presence of extreme anguish. Chapman, also quoted in Chapter 1, declares that tragedy is primarily a thing of moral purpose, encouraging us to cultivate the good and avoid the contrary. The term was often used in a very loose way: Tourneur's *The Atheist's Tragedy* (1611) has its name only from showing the fall of an atheist, and in that respect is at one with medieval usage; Beaumont and Fletcher can use the title *The Maid's Tragedy* (c. 1610) because the girl Aspatia, who is not the main figure, is to make a special impact through her pathos, in being rejected by Amintor, and through her death at his hand.

In the English Renaissance there were a number of plays, not written for the popular theatre but either for the Inns of Court or university stages or for reading alone, which imitated Seneca (or his French imitators) and stressed the horror of the world and the desirability of leaving it. Fulke Greville could write for his Chorus of Priests in *Mustapha* (c. 1596):

> Oh wearisome Condition of Humanity!
> Borne under one Law, to another bound:
> Vainely begot, and yet forbidden vanity;
> Created sicke, commanded to be sound:
> What meaneth Nature by these diverse Lawes?
> Passion and Reason, selfe-division cause:
> Is it the marke or Majesty of Power
> To make offences that it may forgive?
> Nature herselfe doth her owne selfe defloure,
> To hate those errours she her selfe doth give.
> For how should man thinke that, he may not doe
> If Nature did not faile, and punish too?
> Tyrant to others, to her selfe unjust,
> Onely commands things difficult and hard;
> Forbids us all things which it knowes is lust,
> Makes easie paines, unpossible reward.
> If Nature did not take delight in blood,
> She would have made more easie wayes to good.

These are deliberate writings, strongly dependent on antiquity, not the stuff of contemporary theatre. So in Milton, whose *Samson Agonistes* (1671) stands altogether remote from the possibility of performance in his time, there is a turning back to Aristotle, with a stress on 'catharsis' (see Chapter 4 below) and with a highly formal presentation of the action.

England in its non-popular tragedy was merely following a lead powerfully set by Italy and France. The building of the Teatro

Olimpico at Vicenza in 1584 is the most famous of the Italian attempts to provide an appropriately dignified setting for drama that might take its place along with that of antiquity. It was in sixteenth-century Italy too that a line of theorists from Vida to Castelvetro commented on *The Poetics*, adapted Horace's precepts in his *Ars Poetica*, and prescribed for contemporary writers in a rigorous way that was remote from Aristotle's generally descriptive method. In performance Seneca was brought to the stage, the Greeks were adapted, and new plays showed the same kind of blending of classical influence and modern (or 'romantic') subject-matter that was often to characterize the English Inns of Court plays. The story is not essentially different in France, where the name of Robert Garnier (1534–90), well known in England to learned amateurs at the end of the century, is especially prominent. What we feel is lacking in all of this work is a fresh look at the nature of human experience, together with a freedom from *a priori* 'rules'. There is never anything wrong with a dramatist learning his methods from his predecessors, adapting them of course to his particular purposes: Ibsen could learn from the Greeks as well as from the 'well-made play'; Brecht could learn from the Elizabethans. But the Renaissance degree of reverence for the tragedy of antiquity was so great that for a long time the dramatists could see and present the human condition merely as it was presented to them in mirrors that other men had made for the reflection of a vision appropriate only to their time and place. The change at length came in France with Pierre Corneille, in England rather earlier with Marlowe and Shakespeare.

There is a measure of tragic grandeur in Corneille and something altogether surer in Racine. D. D. Raphael has, with force, argued that it was Racine's Jansenism that made it possible for him to see man in a tragic situation, caught up in a universe which he could not strive against, exercising his will yet unable to enforce it, brought up thus against a power he could not resist yet able in his defeat to demonstrate his status as a man (*The Paradox of Tragedy*, 1960, pp. 61–8). Certainly we find Racine giving us what we feel to be tragedy today – in *Andromaque*, in *Phèdre*, even in the bloodless *Bérénice*. For all its difference in style and form, Racine's work gives us an analogue to the major English tragedies of the seventeenth century. He is far more concerned with theory than any of the English writers except Jonson and Chapman, but he is at one with the English in his basic vision of the human situation and his concern with its mystery.

In Spain during this time the matter was different. The dramatists not only adhered to the church's doctrine but wrote their *autos sacramentales* (allegorical plays related to the English 'moralities' but having at their best an authority and an elaborateness of their own) along with their plays for the secular theatre. It was the basic standpoint of the secular plays that ultimately all things could be well if men heeded God's message to them. There was, of course, an occasional note of rebellion, such as shows itself, I believe, in Tirso de Molina's *El Burlador de Sevilla*. It may be heard also perhaps in Calderón's *The Painter of Dishonour*, and it comes near to dominance, with a consequent achievement of a full tragic effect, in his *The Mayor of Zalamea*, where the romantic atmosphere of the play's first scenes is suddenly changed for the darkness of rape and capital punishment. There is nothing explicit to suggest that we are seeing anything but a story of sin and its punishment, but we may be reluctant to tolerate either the girl's rape or the rapist's execution as simple examples of how things must happen on this earth. It is one of the most poignant plays of the seventeenth century, one of the most disturbing too. When I saw it at the Schiller Theater in Berlin a few years ago, my companion (to whom the play was new) could not believe that it would end as it does: the sense of shock when the atmosphere changes is similar to that in Lope de Vega's *The Knight from Olmeda*. 'How can these things be?' is the question that urges itself on us, as in

King Lear the king is made to ask: 'Is there any cause in nature that makes these hard hearts?'

When we come back to England in the late seventeenth century, we find tragedy trying to cope with the idea of 'poetical justice', first presented by Rymer (as quoted in Chapter 1), echoed by Dryden and rebutted by Addison (both quoted there), but nevertheless long-lived, as illustrated by Lewis Theobald in his edition of Shakespeare (1733), where it is argued that the plot of *Hamlet* was well enough because the Prince did after all kill Claudius and so, at least in some measure, merited his death. Although, however, the term is English, the idea is expressed in Racine's preface to *Phèdre* (1672):

> Ce que je puis assurer, c'est que j'en ai point fait où la vertu soit plus mis en jour que dans celle-ci. Les moindres fautes y sont sevèrement punies: la seule pensée du crime y est regardée avec autant d'horreur que le crime même: les faiblesses de l'amour y passent pour de vraies faiblesses: les passions n'y sont présentées aux yeux que pour montrer tout le désordre dont elles sont cause; et le vice y est peint partout avec des couleurs qui en font connaître et haïr la difformité. C'est là proprement le but que tout homme qui travaille pour le public doït se proposer; et c'est que les premiers poëtes tragiques avaient eu en vue sur toute chose. Leur théâtre était une école où la vertu n'était pas moins bien enseignée que dans les écoles des philosophes. [What I can give assurance of is that I have not elsewhere put virtue forth more clearly than here. The slightest faults are here severely punished; the very thought of crime is here regarded with as much horror as crime itself; the weaknesses of love are here shown truly as weaknesses; the passions are presented to the view only to show the total disorder that they cause; and vice is here depicted everywhere so as to make one recognize and hate its deformity. This is indeed the proper end that anyone who works for the public must propose to himself, and it is this that the earliest tragic poets have primarily had in mind. Their theatre was a school where virtue was taught no less than in the schools of the philosophers.]

Nevertheless, Racine wrote tragedy in spite of his theory.

None of the commentators in the eighteenth century thought in terms of a 'tragic sense of life': this was a development of the nineteenth century, implicit perhaps in Coleridge (who thought he had a 'smack of Hamlet' in him, and, if so, how could such a man escape destruction?), but not overt until Hegel and Kierkegaard and Nietzsche had laid the foundations for a new attitude. It was appropriately German and Scandinavian philosophers who gave to tragedy the status, though not necessarily the interpretation, we now associate with it, for Germany came closest in the late eighteenth and early nineteenth centuries to giving us major tragic drama again, and then in the late nineteenth century Ibsen in Norway and Strindberg in Sweden achieved it as fully as any writer in modern times. There is something provisional, however, in Goethe's and Schiller's handlings of tragic themes, something which suggests either bravura (as in Schiller's *Maria Stuart*) or a desire to go 'beyond tragedy' (as Goethe made it evident in his Part II of *Faust*). But soon Georg Büchner in *Danton's Death* (published 1835) and *Wozzeck* (published 1879) made it evident that tragedy was coming to a new birth. Kleist, too, in *Penthesilea* (1808) and *The Prince of Homburg* (1811) showed how a dramatist of his time could embody the idea that man finds himself unable to stand against the powers that confront him. It is surely an error to regard *The Prince of Homburg* as too closely dependent on an exaltation of the Prussian state: the Prince has made for himself an intolerable future in trying to find a way out from the death that threatens him; his final letting-off has to be seen as painful, as a poor substitute for the acceptance of death that he ought to have managed but, like many of us, could not.

No comment on tragic drama can disregard Ibsen's *Brand* and *Hedda Gabler* and *John Gabriel Borkman* or Strindberg's *The Father* and *Miss Julie*. Like Euripides, both dramatists moved away at times into ironic comedy and wrote some of their major plays in that Kind: Ibsen's *Peer Gynt* and *The Wild Duck*, Strindberg's

Creditors, for example. But Strindberg's later manner belonged in neither of these Kinds, but rather in a new fantastic mode exemplified at its highest in *The Ghost Sonata* and *A Dream Play*, or in a specially anguished drama that looked for peace at the close and hesitatingly affirmed it, most obviously in *The Dance of Death*, which has affiliations with Ibsen's *Little Eyolf*. All these are major plays, indeed are among the special triumphs of the modern theatre, and they stand not only apart from but strikingly above those Ibsen plays where the influence of Kierkegaard was most evident. *Peer Gynt* is a splendid exercise of the imagination, though even there the presence of the Danish philosopher is felt so strongly that at times we feel we are in the world of the preacher's *exemplum*: like the writer of a moral play in medieval times, Ibsen here illustrates a doctrine he has absorbed. But *An Enemy of the People* and *The Lady from the Sea* (fascinating as a document though this indeed is) are on a lower level, asserting too strenuously the need to 'break through' the general, imposed pattern of life and thus win freedom by choosing 'on one's own responsibility': in these instances the doctrine seems too deliberately embraced. Both dramatists contribute most strongly to the tragic Kind when they are governed by an intuition of what living at its most crucial moments is, and are furthest from theorizing about it.

Nevertheless, the change in philosophical approach to which these tragedies can be related was of major importance in modern thinking and served to give tragic writing a basis, no longer in a mere tradition where the term 'tragedy' had been so variously applied, but in conceptions of human life intimately associated with the consciousness of the time. The 'tragic sense of life' – in Hegel, in Kierkegaard, in Nietzsche – goes quite beyond the idea of didacticism, which was the official Renaissance view, quite beyond the idea of 'poetical justice', which remained (despite Addison's objection) in the eighteenth century, quite beyond Goethe's or Coleridge's view of Hamlet (the plant in the fragile vase, the man too thoughtful for the world). It implies, rather, that our situation is necessarily tragic, that all men exist in an evil situation and, if they are aware, are anguished because they are aware. Hegel emphasized a necessary opposition of forces dividing man from man and man from himself, Kierkegaard a desperate need for man to break out from an imposed pattern, Nietzsche the joy that can come when in tragic writing Dionysus and Apollo are made to dwell together. And of course these writers are far from being alone: Miguel de Unamuno and Karl Jaspers are perhaps only the most obvious among more recent names to add. (For useful extracts from the philosophical writings on the subject, see the anthologies edited by Laurence Michel and Richard B. Sewall and by Robert W. Corrigan, both included in the bibliography at the end of this book.) So new is all this that we can say that the concept of tragedy, as it is now generally understood, is a creation of the last two centuries, even though our contemporary theatre has shown more than a little caution in its approach to tragedy as a dramatic Kind. We may ask, Who really 'worried' about tragedy before the nineteenth century? Until then it was simply respected. The worry has in some measure inhibited the dramatists.

Yet it is by no means universally accepted that, despite many and obvious differences, all 'true' tragedies are at one in implying a particular view of man's condition. J. C. Maxwell, for example, in his note 'The Presuppositions of Tragedy' (*Essays in Criticism*, V (1955), 175–8) has argued that to believe that there is a 'tragic view of things' is to place tragedy unwarrantably 'on a separate footing from the other main literary forms'. Certainly it is not only possible but altogether necessary that tragic plays should be critically examined in relation to what distinguishes them from one another, not merely in relation to the Kind they belong to: the preoccupation with Kind – an enforced preoccupation in this present book – can exercise an inhibiting and debilitating influence on our concern with the nature of the individual work. *Hamlet* and *Lear*, the *Oresteia* and the *Antigone*, *Phèdre* and *The Duchess of Malfi*, exist in a way that 'Tragedy' does not. 'Tragedy' is today a concept that we deduce from the contemplation of a heap of tragedies. For the Greeks and the men of the Renaissance, it was something different partly because their range of examples was different. We have exalted the term into a concept underlying works that differ perhaps in all ways except in embodying that concept. It is good that from time to time a critic should say, as Nicholas Brooke does at the beginning of his book *Shakespeare's Early Tragedies* (1968): 'I have no general theory of Tragedy to propound. In fact, rather the reverse. It seems to me that within the very loose term "tragedy" there is a range of possibility, of positive variety, such as we expect to find in "comedy"' (p. 3). From such an approach it is likely that we shall get some of the sharpest insights into individual writings – as indeed often happens when the most thorough and persistent schematizers set their schemes aside for a while. We have in Proust an insistence on the particular work's uniqueness:

> So it is that a well-read man will at once begin to yawn with boredom when anyone speaks to him of a new 'good book', because he imagines a sort of composite of all the good books that he has read and knows already, whereas a good book is something special, something incalculable, and is made up not of the sum of all previous masterpieces but of something which the most thorough assimilation of every one of them would not enable him to discover, since it exists not in their sum but beyond it. Once he has become acquainted with this new work, the well-read man, till then apathetic, feels his interest awaken in the reality which it depicts.
>
> (*Within a Budding Grove*, translated by C. K. Scott Moncrieff, reprinted 1967, Vol. I, p. 327)

Characteristically, this comment on books arises out of a consideration of the uniqueness of each individual girl: the analogy is justified, for the vital encounter with a book new to us has some of the characteristics of a love-affair. We may add that each new work in any recognizable Kind modifies to some degree our conception of that Kind. Frank Kermode has remarked: 'when you hear talk of archetypes, reach for your reality principle' (*Continuities*, New York, 1968, p. 121). We should also reach for it when we are reading a book on 'Tragedy'. Even so, since the beginning of a philosophical concern with tragedy in the nineteenth century, a sense of what a writer is doing when he undertakes what we agree to call a 'tragedy' can sharpen the impact of the individual work – so long as we avoid an easy equation of one such work with another.

Many people wrote what they called tragedies in the years following the seventeenth century, with the ancient or Renaissance examples still dominant on their thought. The eighteenth century had many plays in blank verse set in Greek or Roman times and ending in disaster. So too did the nineteenth century, far more than most people realize. All the major Romantic and Victorian poets made an attempt at rivalling Shakespeare: Shelley with considerable but intermittent power in *The Cenci* (1818), Byron more than creditably in some of his plays: Wordsworth and Coleridge had preceded them; Beddoes, Tennyson, Browning, Swinburne followed. All wanted to give to their time dramatic writings that could endure the comparison with Shakespeare; most of them (but not always Byron) cultivated a Shakespearian idiom. Only Beddoes made the idiom vital by giving it a new and individual imprint, and his plays were remote from the possibility of performance in his time. This pattern of things continued into the last years of the nineteenth century and the first years of the twentieth – for example, in the writings of Stephen Phillips – although there were dramatists, like Gordon Bottomley and T. S. Eliot, who tried to escape from the tyranny of the blank-verse line and the Elizabethan atmosphere. What they always lacked was a sufficient sense of the pressure of the ways things are.

In Ireland things were rather different. The Abbey Theatre arose out of the desire for a national drama rooted in still powerful myth and giving to Ireland the kind of ritual enactment of its past that Hellas had known on the tragic stage. The at first dominant impulse, that given by Yeats, achieved its finest realization in Yeats's own *Deirdre* (1907), but the theatre turned away from verse to prose in Synge's *R?ers to the Sea* (1904) and *Deirdre of the Sorrows* (acted in 1910 after Synge's death). It also turned much more to comedy than Yeats can have expected, but we shall note later its remarkable return to declared tragedy in the early plays of O'Casey. For its best writing in this Kind, we can see Dublin as the one place in the earliest years of this century where tragedy in the English language was boldly and simply essayed and firmly achieved.

In recent years dramatists in England and elsewhere have been more modest, and yet have on occasion come nearer to a sense of the tragic than was common in the two hundred years preceding. We do not find the words 'A Tragedy' on a title-page today, yet again and again dramatists have retold the ancient stories and have adapted them to a contemporary or near-contemporary setting or have interpreted them, while keeping to the original place and time, in the light of contemporary thought. So in France André Obey employed the Iphigenia in Aulis theme in his *Une Fille pour du vent* (1953); Jean Anouilh wrote a *Medea* (1946) and an *Antigone* (1944), respectively probing into Medea's psychological state and seeing the Creon-Antigone opposition in relation to France under the German occupation; Jean-Paul Sartre in *Les Mouches (The Flies,* 1943) presented Orestes as existentialist man. In the United States, Eugene O'Neill took the *Oresteia* as the ground-plan for *Mourning Becomes Electra* (1931), writing it as a trilogy with each part having a fairly close relation to the corresponding part in

Aeschylus. In England it was the *Oresteia* again that gave T. S. Eliot his cue for *The Family Reunion* (1939), though his treatment was altogether freer than O'Neill's and was Christian in its viewpoint while O'Neill was psychoanalytic. Eliot went on to use plays by Euripides and Sophocles for the provision of similar cues for his own work. Other dramatists have sought a comparable authority by taking stories from history and legend, as we have seen in Yeats's and Synge's treatments of the Deirdre story, as also in Albert Camus's *Caligula* (1945), Jean Giraudoux' *La Guerre de Troie n'aura pas lieu* (1935, translated as *Tiger at the Gates*), Anouilh's *Eurydice* (1941, translated as *Point of Departure*), Maxwell Anderson's series of blank verse plays on English, American and continental European historical themes. Apart from Eliot and Anderson, these dramatists have used prose but have sought for a high seriousness in their effect through the authority that our memories of the ancient (or some other past) world have given to their action. This can be a dangerous undertaking, for we are likely, especially when Greek plays are thus used, to make damaging comparisons. Apart, however, from the fact that the attempt to draw on the past in this way shows an urge to achieve tragic writing in our time, it has also to be recognized that this group of plays includes some of the best, as well as some of the most disappointing, drama of this century. *Deirdre of the Sorrows, Les Mouches, Mourning Becomes Electra, Eurydice* have to be included in any short list of the best plays since the careers of Ibsen and Strindberg and Chekhov came to an end.

The practice of course was not new. From the Renaissance onwards Greek themes have been re-employed, in Italy, in France, in England. One of the sixteenth-century Inns of Court dramas was a *Jocasta* by George Gascoigne and Francis Kinwelmersh (1566), adapted from an Italian version of Euripides' *Phoenissae*; Dryden and Nathaniel Lee wrote an *Oedipus* (1678); Roman history and Greek legend provided the material for tragic plays from Shakespeare and Jonson down to Swinburne. In Chapter IX of *The Poetics* Aristotle said there was nothing inherently wrong in a dramatist's employment of an invented story, and some of the plays in the Greek theatre, he said, did so; but he added that there was an advantage in using one of the traditional plots in that, if the audience know that the play's incidents have actually occurred, they can the more easily believe in what they are seeing. We might perhaps rather put it that the story which has powerful associations for us, either through our having already responded to it in a masterwork or through our knowing it as a part, probably a major part, in the actual or legendary history of mankind, will start off with the advantage of such associations. The dramatist may aim, however, at a deliberate variation in mood, as in Jean Cocteau's *La Machine infernale* (1934) or André Gide's *Oedipus* (published 1930), in both of which the Oedipus story is presented in a muted and sometimes comic fashion. In such instances the force of the treatment may be the greater through the very shock of the variation.

Nevertheless, this cleaving to past event and to what already has its place in past theatre has not given us the drama of strongest impact in the twentieth century. Not Ibsen and Strindberg in their tragic plays, not the Greeks, have been the most powerful of influences on the dramatists of our time. Rather it has been Strindberg in the mode of *The Ghost Sonata*, leading on to Frank Wedekind, the German expressionists, and Bertolt Brecht; it has been Shaw, who began as a quasi-Ibsenite writer of social drama, moved to an ironic variant on the society comedies of the late nineteenth century, and thence, from *Back to Methusaleh* (1919–20) onwards, to a kind of extravaganza, cartoon drama which exhibited the world's strangeness and folly while letting it appear that there was at least a kind of wisdom available if man cared to use it; it has been Chekhov too, who refused the title of 'tragedy' to any of his plays yet, more than any other dramatist of recent times, has sympathetically portrayed the condition of lost hope. We may especially note the remarkable endings in *anagnorisis* (see Chapter 6 below) of *Uncle Vanya* (1899) and *The Three Sisters* (1901), but it is useful to observe the connection between his writing as a whole and much of the work that is currently being done. That there is a tragic element in Harold Pinter's *The Caretaker* (1960), in John McGrath's *Events while guarding the Bofors Gun* (1966), in Tom Stoppard's *Rosencrantz and Guildenstern are Dead* (1966) is a matter I shall want to suggest in Chapter 8. But all three plays, by no means equal in accomplishment or similar in method, are alike in deliberately eschewing the tragic manner. Stoppard's makes fun of the *Hamlet* it recalls, Pinter's has affiliations with Strindberg at his non-naturalistic extreme and on the other hand cultivates a comic response in much of its dialogue, McGrath's seems to offer a 'slice of life' and apparently (only apparently) leave it at that. It is as if these dramatists, while responding to the human situation in a way which we can call 'tragic' in the traditional sense and which has manifest relations with philosophic thought on the tragic condition, refuse to set themselves up as tragic writers, refrain from appearing to offer the minimal affirmations that are basic in tragedy. Tragedy here, as characteristically in drama of the 1960s, is an undercurrent but, I believe, a determining one.

Yet we need to observe briefly a notable exception, though one that is already some time away from us. The major dramas of Federigo García Lorca (1899–1936) have a tragic simplicity and wholeness that is closer perhaps to the dominant quality in Yeats and Synge than to anything else in twentieth-century writing. Under Spain's bright sun, on Spain's dry and disputed earth, a tragic poet showed us human beings living the more fully because of the walls that shut them in. These plays will always be difficult to act in climates remote from Lorca's, but they indicate supremely that tragedy belongs to the twentieth-century theatre as surely as it has belonged to any other.

Not merely in the drama, however, has the tragic note been heard. Aristotle in Chapter V of *The Poetics* declared that tragedy and epic were close in the 'objects' of their 'imitation' – that is, they presented the same kind of materials but in different manners. This was not original with him, for Plato in *The Republic* commonly associated Homer with the writers of tragedy. Nor is Aristotle consistent on the point, for in Chapter XIII he says that *The Odyssey*, in finally bringing good fortune to the good and bad to the bad, offered a pleasure near to that of comedy. Nevertheless, his general view is that tragedy differs from epic primarily in being intended for performance in a theatre. For Aristotle, such performance was a comparatively minor matter – a view in which we are not likely to follow him (see Chapter 4 below) – but we can understand his position better if we remember both the practice of recitation of non-dramatic poetry in ancient Greece and the fact that only a few tragedies, out of the many written, could achieve the distinction of performance in Greek theatres. Moreover, we can see that *The Iliad* especially has at certain moments an effect almost marginally separate from the tragic when tragedy is read rather than performed. The death of Hector, the visit of Priam to Achilles when he begs permission to give funeral rites to his son's body, the sitting together of the two men when Achilles' consent is won – these are things out of which tragedy is made. Where epic and tragedy essentially differ, apart from the fact of performance, is that in epic we have 'tragic moments' in a context which is characterized by amplitude and variety rather than concentration and crisis. So it is with the modern novel, which almost began with Richardson's *Clarissa Harlowe* (1747–48), enormous in length but concentrated on the fate of a single figure who comes to humiliation and death and, through that very fact, is enabled to assert a human dignity which would not have been within her compass if her life had had the more even tenor to be expected for a girl of her station in that time. Intermittently since then, despite the preponderating influence of Richardson's contemporary Fielding, who declared the novel to be essentially 'a comic epic poem in prose', the novel has used a theme and a structure comparable with those of tragic drama. Stendhal's *Le Rouge et le Noir* (1831), Flaubert's *Madame Bovary* (1856), Melville's *Moby Dick* (1851) and *Billy Budd* (published 1924), Hawthorne's *The Scarlet Letter* (1850), Tolstoy's *Anna Karenina* (1875–76), Hardy's *Tess of the D'Urbervilles* (1891) and *Jude the Obscure* (1895), Conrad's *Lord Jim* (1900) and *Nostromo* (1904), are among the examples that come most readily to mind, but it is customary indeed to speak of a 'sense of the tragic' in Henry James, and as recently as 1947 Malcolm Lowry's *Under the Volcano* was manifestly directed towards tragedy, keeping (after Chapter 1) to the Renaissance Unities of Time and Place in order to secure that concentration of effect, that sense of a doom always only a few hours away, that T. S. Eliot in *The Use of Poetry and the Use of Criticism* (1933) saw as being a source of special strength, though of course not a necessity: this matter will be returned to in Chapter 7. Before that, André Malraux had written *La Condition humaine* (1933) and *L'Espoir* (1938), Albert Camus *L'Etranger* (1942) and *La Peste* (1947) – all of them novels which have given to our time a full sense of what it is to live in a tragic situation.

Yet it is not our custom to describe these works as 'tragedies': we say they are tragic novels. The noun is still, in precise usage, restricted to the drama – for reasons that we shall see are not merely historical. It may well be that at some future time it will be the nineteenth- and twentieth-century novel that is recognized as embodying more profoundly, in certain cases, the tragic spirit than the drama of these years has done. But for us, as yet, tragedy is something acted or at least written for acting.

During the twentieth century writing *on*, as distinct from *of*, tragedy has been abundant. A. C. Bradley's *Shakespearean Tragedy*

(1904) was not merely a summation of nineteenth-century criticism of Shakespeare: it was also a book that aimed at a serious and
profound consideration of the nature of tragic art. Strangely, it
almost wholly neglected the theatre and paid little attention to the
force of Shakespeare's words, but its author saw the plays as con-
stituting a statement on how a major tragic dramatist confronted
the human condition when he was writing. Since Bradley's time
there have been innumerable books and articles on the tragedies of
the past, and only a very small (perhaps somewhat arbitrary)
selection can be included in the bibliography at the end of this
book. Tragedy has never been more fully studied as a genre, as a
way of presenting the world, than it has been during this century.
Or, indeed, as we have seen, more desperately worried about.
Freud used Oedipus and Orestes as type-names for recurrent, or
perhaps even universal, complexes. The dramatists, we have noted,
have frequently run the risk of re-telling the stories that the Greeks
themselves used. Shakespeare can be rehandled by Tom Stoppard.
And in universities everywhere there is earnest discussion on
whether 'tragedy' can now be written. It would not be so earnest if
there were not a feeling that a civilization without tragedy is
dangerously lacking something. In the chapters that follow, it will
be suggested that tragedy, as it can exist today, must be very
different in manner from the plays we have from Sophocles or
Shakespeare or Racine, but that in its essence it will be at one with
them.

This chapter has given only a series of glimpses of what tragedy
has meant in Europe through the ages. Omissions may be seen in
plenty, but what has been aimed at is to present the continuing
preoccupation with the tragic, and the variety of shapes that tragic
writing – and of writing about tragedy – has taken.

3
The Tragic Hero

Aristotle, we have seen, recommended but did not insist on the use of the traditional stories in tragedy: the practice entailed that the central place was normally given to heroes and kings. Moreover, he laid it down as inherent in tragedy that the personages must be 'better than we are', which S. H. Butcher in *Aristotle's Theory of Poetry and Fine Art* (1894) interpreted as more fully 'organized', further along in the path of nature's realization of itself, than is possible in the ordinarily confused human condition. This statement comes in Chapter II: much later, in Chapter XXV, he seems to give special credit to Sophocles (as distinct from Euripides) for presenting 'things as they ought to be'. We can link this with what Sidney says in *An Apology for Poetry* on the 'golden world' which poetry presents: it is not a world where everything is good, but a world where things exist in a pure rather than a mixed form. What is important is the sense of full, or at least unusual, realization of the powers and tendencies peculiar to man. Orestes kills his mother, Oedipus marries his mother and kills his father, Medea kills her children: yet they are, in a sense, more fully themselves than men and women usually dare to be. It must be remembered, too, that in the Greek theatre the actor was a remote figure, masked, wearing *cothurnoi* on his feet and an *onkos* on his head (so that he had a height of some seven and a half feet), and was taking part in a religious and civic rite at a special festival. He stood for the people – indeed, it will be seen in Chapter 4 that he was in an important sense their victim – but he was representing a king or hero, he spoke with a poet's majestic words, he was manifestly doomed. He necessarily induced awe, a sense of being 'above' even as he fell.

The picture was modified in those plays of Euripides where the tragic form was employed to accommodate a sceptical spirit, as in the plays noted briefly in Chapter 2. But the basic concept remained through the ancient world. When there was a protagonist – and we shall see in a moment that that was not always the case, at least throughout a play or trilogy – he was of exalted rank and held, for this and other reasons, a position of recognizable eminence. Certainly this was how it was in Seneca. His central figures are men in high place: as a stoic philosopher he knows that this is an evil thing, that what matters is that one shall be king over oneself, that this is rendered more difficult when one has the relation with men that power entails: that, for him, is the mainspring of tragedy. And when in the Middle Ages the idea of tragedy came for a time to be divorced from play-writing, we can see in the quotations from Diomedes and Isidore of Seville and Chaucer in Chapter 1 that there continues to be a stress on 'heroic characters', 'commonwealths and kings', 'heigh degree'. So in the quotation there given from Sidney we see that in the Renaissance the concept did not in this respect change: tragedy is a warning to tyrants, but it is also something that stirs us, the spectators, to 'admiration' as well as 'commiseration'. The practice of the Renaissance was not basically different from its theory. Shakespeare is bold in making a mere general his hero in *Othello*, and similar compromises with greatness are common in the plays of Beaumont and Fletcher in the years that followed. Still, they are only compromises: these men do occupy high place. The hero is normally a king or prince, either by right of birth or through conquest or usurpation, as in Marlowe's *Tamburlaine* and Shakespeare's *Macbeth*, or he is a man who in other ways wins peculiar power, as in *Doctor Faustus*. Always he has a fall to endure. Elizabethan-Jacobean drama does include a few plays that strain after the tragic effect in a purely domestic setting, as in the anonymous *Arden of Feversham* (c. 1591) and in Thomas Heywood's *A Woman Killed with Kindness* (1603) and *The English Traveller* (c. 1625), but Heywood avoided the claim that he was writing 'tragedy' here. We can safely say that dramatic tragedy from antiquity to the nineteenth century normally implied a concern with people in high place. In the preceding section, however, we have seen that the novel, from Richardson onwards, approaches a sense of the tragic not at all infrequently, and the novel has only exceptionally had kings and princes in the central position. If for no other reason, the drama was bound to be affected. But of course there were other reasons. Kings and princes have become less important throughout the world: a sovereign reigns but now hardly ever rules; his position is reduced so thoroughly to the symbolic that it is a burden that many men think should not be inflicted on a human being. 'Great place' there can still be, for the occasional prime minister or president or dictator, but in the present half-century such men can be quickly numbered through.

It can be argued that this is a major loss to tragedy. If a king falls, a nation is affected. The opening lines of *I Henry VI* indicate a sense that with Henry V's death England has suffered disaster:

> Hung be the heavens with black, yield day to night!
> Comets, importing change of time and states,
> Brandish your crystal tresses in the sky
> And with them scourge the bad revolting stars
> That have consented unto Henry's death!
> King Henry the Fifth, too famous to live long!
> England ne'er lost a king of so much worth.
>
> (I. i. 1–7)

Yet we do not really find much of this in tragedy. Hamlet is regretted because 'he was likely, had he been put on,/To have prov'd most royal', but Fortinbras is securely in charge of Denmark and we may feel is more likely to be the efficient monarch. The end of

King Lear is a lament for Lear's death and suffering, but no hint is there that Britain's future is in danger: it will probably be safer under the mediocre and fumbling Albany than under the irascible and wayward old king. Macbeth and Tamburlaine, however much we are involved (and indeed we are greatly involved) in their fortunes, cannot be regretted as rulers. Webster in *The White Devil* and *The Duchess of Malfi* goes out of his way to suggest, rather anticlimactically, that things can now be put in better shape. Jonson's *Sejanus* and *Catiline* and Shakespeare's *Antony and Cleopatra* and *Coriolanus* tells us the stories of men who abused their gifts: we have no enthusiasm for Octavius or Tiberius, or for the Roman state in general as it is presented in these plays, but we cannot feel that the heroes' deaths have endangered the welfare of the people.

Yet of course it is a dramatic convenience if the central figure is given a position of manifest eminence. He will appear to have a special claim to our attention, and, we shall see in Chapter 4, a special claim to be our victim. But in contemporary writing, unless we go back to the past for our material, we have not enough candidates for the position. In our scheme of things, the higher the eminence, the greater the responsibility and the more restricted the power. A shop steward or a students' leader (lacking major responsibility) can exercise authority more easily than a prime minister, a president of a business firm or a university. This seems indeed to be increasingly the situation even with princes of the church. In the drama, as for a long time in the novel, we now have ordinary men as heroes, for almost all the extraordinary men live in private life and are therefore in that sense ordinary. They may, none the less, when brought to the stage or the pages of a novel, stay more firmly in our minds than men in apparently more prominent places.

Nor, if the dramatist is fit for the task of tragedy, does it ultimately matter. He has to give us the sense of the privately extraordinary. He may take a brace of attendant lords, as in *Rosencrantz and Guildenstern are Dead*, but give them a growing awareness of the way things are in the human condition – that is, bring them, as we shall note in Chapter 6, to a point of *anagnorisis* – and thus compel us to see them as reaching a point that we cannot imagine ourselves surpassing. He may take an obscure revolutionary like Katow in Malraux's novel *La Condition humaine* and give to him not only a degree of authority through the quiet dignity he has throughout the book but also a quite exceptional status as he confronts the terrible death which, but for a moment of the purest charity, he could have avoided. Or his choice may be Melville's Billy Budd, an almost illiterate and uncomprehending sailor, whose devotion to truth and simple virtue takes our breath away while not (for a wonder) inducing incredulity. Or he may do as O'Casey did, defying current practice by using the description 'tragedy' for *The Shadow of a Gunman* (1923), *Juno and the Paycock* (1924) and *The Plough and the Stars* (1926) and yet having as his central figures people who lived much as other people have done but who gained special eminence through the totality of their devotion. In all three plays Juno is the only character who is allowed a long speech showing her awareness of what is happening and its larger implications. O'Casey grew more cautious later: *The Silver Tassie* (published 1928) is called a 'tragi-comedy', and he withholds the term 'tragedy' even from *Red Roses for Me* (published 1943). But we can recognize him as outstanding among those playwrights who have written tragically about the common man, the man who, in Bywater's translation of Aristotle, is described as being almost 'just as we are': for Aristotle, that implied a middle way of writing which he did not see as belonging to either tragedy or comedy, but this middle way is referred to only incidentally in *The Poetics*.

Yet there must, I think, be some sense of eminence if the tragic writer depends on a central figure. It may be, as I have suggested, through the sharpness of the revelation, the *anagnorisis*; it may be through the particularity of the distress, or through the possession of a special virtue and dignity. Hence the doubts that some of us have had about Falder in Galsworthy's *Justice* (1910) and Willie Loman in Arthur Miller's *Death of a Salesman* (1949). Both of these figures come to desperation, but neither seems to know more at the end than at the beginning, neither seems 'notable' in the sense that we need from a tragic figure. Willie's wife Linda exhorts us: 'But he's a human being, and a terrible thing is happening to him. So attention must be paid.' We have to agree, but our concern is sociological rather than with Willie as an *essential* human being: he is the victim of the American dream rather than of the human condition.

A fall there always is, and the tragic writer is inevitably concerned with how it operates. Aristotle, in one of the passages from *The Poetics* given in Chapter 1, insisted that it came through '*hamartia*', an error of judgement which allowed disaster in. This has been usually interpreted as involving a kind of 'poetical justice' from Thomas Rymer on (though often with more qualification than Rymer allowed), as the result of a 'fatal imperfection or error', as Bradley put it. Aristotle rejected the notion of an evil or a totally good hero: the one would not move us to pity, he said; the fall of the other would merely shock us. This overlooks the oneness we can feel with a Richard of Gloucester, the sense of recognition of a truth that we get when Billy Budd perishes. Both these figures in their ways amaze us (as Katow does in *La Condition humaine*), but each is close enough to us for a sense of kinship to develop, each makes us aware of a common fatality. What is necessary is that we should feel the interrelation of character and circumstance. 'Poetical justice' is simply not found in tragedy, where Cordelia is hanged, Ophelia drowned, Othello driven to Desdemona's murder, Lear to madness. But all these characters act in such a way as to contribute to a developing process of event which will ultimately include their personal disasters. Billy Budd strikes Claggart: 'Struck dead by an angel of God. But the angel must hang,' says Captain Vere, Melville's other tragic figure in the story. Billy is not guilty, even though Randall Stewart has argued that his stammer is a sign of Original Sin, a verdict that might have astonished Melville ('The Vision of Evil in Hawthorne and Melville', *The Tragic Vision and the Christian Faith*, edited by Nathan A. Scott, Jr., New York, 1957, pp. 238–63). The whole process that tragedy shows is one in which man plays his part: we cannot know how large that part is; we may suspect it to be small (as probably Aristotle did when he urged on the dramatist who used an event of apparent chance, like the falling of a statue to kill a man, the need to make it at least appear appropriate); we must nevertheless, if we are writing tragedy, give some credence to the idea that men somehow contribute to what happens.

In talking of tragedy, perhaps we should avoid the term 'free will' and use rather the idea of participation in the encompassing process which would not be quite the same if we were not here to act and think and feel. In this indeed there is an aesthetic problem – that of reconciling the sense of human vitality with the sense of a prepared disaster. In almost every tragedy the atmosphere is one of doom from the beginning. *Romeo and Juliet* might have appeared from its opening scenes to have a reasonable chance of ending happily, but Shakespeare has given us a prologue to assure us that it will not, and has put foreboding words in Romeo's mouth as he goes to the Capulets' house to meet Juliet for the first time and into Juliet's in the first balcony-scene. Calderón's *The Mayor of Zalamea* takes a sudden dive to disaster when the act of rape follows on an evening spent in an atmosphere of civilized hospitality, but we have seen that Calderón, though 'tragic moments' belong to his dramas as they do to the epic and the novel, is overtly demonstrating sin and punishment according to God's scheme, not that unavoidable and irredeemable ill which we must consider in Chapter 4. Among more recent examples of tragedies that take us by surprise the most notable is *Juno and the Paycock*, where O'Casey in Act I only hints at the devastation he will later present, and meanwhile stresses, with apparent good nature, the laughable element in human conduct. The general procedure is to show from the beginning that things will not be well. The ghost in the first scene of *Hamlet*, the appearance of Iago at the very beginning of *Othello*, the Witches that open *Macbeth*, the folly and arrogance of Lear on his first appearance – all these are as clearly determining as the speech of Dionysus at the beginning of the *Bacchae*. Logically we could assume only that what is willed by the characters is itself part of a larger will, of something already 'written'. That would fit Hegel's notion well enough, for he sees the opposition of Creon and Antigone as essentially involved in human relations: they must clash because men living together will necessarily assert both the claim of government and the claim of an overriding intuition of what is right. Aristotle is more cautious: he never speaks of 'necessity' but of 'probability *or* necessity' as being the connective between the events of a tragedy. In the Renaissance, we have seen, tragedy could be regarded by men as diverse as Sidney and Chapman as holding up warning examples, which, if heeded, would save men from error and its penalty. In this they are in some measure followed by those writers of recent years who attempt a reconciliation between tragedy and the Christian faith. Both groups of writers seem to disregard the manifest determinism of the tragic framework as it commonly appears. I have argued elsewhere that tragedy allows a minimal free will in that a particular act sets off the train of events that leads to disaster, that what follows is beyond human control (*Shakespeare's Tragedies and Other Studies in Seventeenth Century Drama*, 1950, p. 16). This is basically the idea expressed in the quotation from Anouilh's *Antigone* given in Chapter 1. On consideration, however, the plan seems too simple a one. Which was the determining act in the long story of the house of Atreus, which the *Oresteia* refers to, from time to time, in retrospect? Was it for Oedipus his rashness in probing the mystery, or his parents' giving him to death, or his attempt to thwart the oracle that told him incest and parricide lay ahead for him? Or was it a decree of the gods that could not be overborne, from long before the time of any man we hear of in the play? Which act of Othello's sealed his doom: his marriage, his passing over of Iago in the matter of promotion, his first heeding of Iago's calumnies? Or was it something in Othello's own nature that doomed him, whatever the particular circumstances of the case? The question of free will remains a highly dubious one in tragic writing. We are shown how things are, or as they appear to be to a writer who, at least for the time being, is seeing man's condition as ultimately inseparable from disaster. But there is included the fact that, perhaps by some supreme irony, perhaps because he is what he is, a sentient being, a man has the experience of himself contributing to the process which involves his end. *Moira*, at least for the later Stoics, was only roughly equivalent to our 'fate': it meant rather the sum total of all things that have been, are, will be; it can be seen as independent of time, independent of the gods, through whom it was none the less mediated to men. William Chase Greene has thus indicated the position of Chrysippus in the third century B.C.: 'All these arguments might be summarized in the proposition that the future is wholly contained in the present, or indeed in the past.' (*Moira: Fate, Good, and Evil in Greek Thought*, reprinted New York and Evanston, 1963, p. 347.) Late as Chrysippus is in relation to extant Greek tragedies, the notion of 'timelessness' seems to underlie most of the major plays. Yet a man could accept, could will, his particular *moira*. In any event, whatever he did, as a sentient being, became part of that totality which was his already written story. H. D. F. Kitto has assured us that in Greek tragedy: 'The gods are a controlling element . . ., but not in what the actors do and suffer: that is entirely their own affair' (*Form and Meaning in Drama*, 1956, p. 244). And this we must accept in that we see

Medea willing and acting out the murder of her children, Pentheus deliberately challenging Dionysus. But it remains evident that in these plays Medea and Pentheus are presented as willed as well as willing: we could not imagine them as acting other than they do, and the gods are prepared for it. No dramatic character seems freer, as we watch, than a Shakespearian hero. Every time we see *Othello*, we feel that *this* time he surely will not be taken in. The theatre always acts doubly on us: it gives us a rehearsed, already written play, but we have the sense that the action is freshly happening before us; a tragedy tells a story that, in nearly every instance, we are fully warned cannot have other than a disastrous ending, yet as Macbeth chooses, as Hamlet plays his tricks, we feel him to be as free as we are. But only 'as free'. Looking back on our own lives, we shall not see that there were neglected alternatives that we could have seized, yet we have a long experience of what it has felt like to 'choose'. In the paradox lies much of tragedy's strength. It reminds us. Wilbur Sanders, in referring to the acceptance of fatalism by Shakespeare's Richard II, has declared that 'Necessity neither requires nor invites cooperation' (*The Dramatist and the Received Idea: Studies in the Plays of Marlowe and Shakespeare*, Cambridge, 1968, p. 180), but this appears to be simplism: the most dreadful thing about 'Necessity' is that we seem after all to have cooperated in its working. In the conduct of a play's action, moreover, there may be incidental things which have the appearance of pure chance, as in Hamlet's killing of Polonius. In retrospect, however, even these seem 'right' for the people concerned: Polonius's spying, evident earlier in his relations with his son, makes him essentially vulnerable to sudden destruction; Hamlet's giving way to hot temper in this scene anticipates the manner in which he will kill Claudius.

It has been possible to dismiss the idea of a simple 'poetical justice' easily enough – not because it does not adhere to nature (we have seen that Rymer, the term's inventor, recognized that fully), but because it does not adhere to the practice of our major writers, from the Greeks to today. But one brief observation must be added. I have doubted Aristotle's pronouncement that a really bad man cannot be a tragic hero (arguing that Macbeth for all his crimes, Richard of Gloucester for all his determination to be a villain, are not outside our sense of humanity's range), and have noted the contribution that a tragic character normally makes to the total process that involves him. What must now be said is that, in major tragedy, the question of degrees of guilt ultimately becomes irrelevant. There has been some unnecessary debating on whether the Duchess of Malfi was 'guilty' in defying 'degree', in paying scant attention to her duchy's welfare, in marrying secretly and for a second time. All these things were regarded at least dubiously in seventeenth-century England. But when we come to her long agony in Act IV of Webster's play, we do not stop to ask about 'desert'. Nor do we in the scenes of humiliation and barely thinkable torment that Marlowe's Edward II endured near the end of his tragedy. Of course, he was a weak and careless king who chose his friends as badly as a man could, who played the tyrant and the puppet alternately with his barons. Marlowe goes to the limit here, perhaps, in arousing the characteristic tragic emotion through a central figure who, for the greater part of the play, is remote from our sympathy and can hardly be said anywhere to win our respect, far less our 'admiration'. Yet in its strange fashion *Edward II* does seem to stay within the tragic Kind. We may indeed say it is a limiting case, though something not altogether dissimilar appears in Arthur Miller's *A View from the Bridge* (1955): different as in all other ways these plays are, they come together in that Edward Plantagenet and Eddie Carbone transcend what they do through the extreme anguish it brings upon them.

We must finally in this section ask whether, or to what extent, tragedy needs a tragic hero. Or the question might for a moment be rephrased: at what point did the idea of a hero enter tragedy?

In Chapter IV of *The Poetics* we read that tragedy, like comedy, began in 'improvisations' ('*ap' archēs autoschedrastēs*'), and Bywater interprets this as meaning:

> Tragedy began when the author of the dithyramb came forward with an 'improvisation', i.e. with a ῥῆσις or spoken statement, which he improvised in the interval between the two halves of the song of the chorus – that being the origin of the two great constituents of a Greek drama, a spoken part and a sung part, an actor and a chorus.
>
> (p. 134)

At that point the actor, as distinct from the chorus, must surely be seen as explicator or narrator, not as the man who in his own person assumes the role of victim. If we examine the *Agamemnon*, moreover, we see that for almost half its length the play is made up of alternations between a single speaker (in turn the Watchman, Clytemnestra, the Herald, Clytemnestra again, the Herald again) and the choral songs. It is true that the Herald is on-stage during Clytemnestra's second speech and that she addresses him, but, as he does not speak in her presence, this is no true duologue. Up to the moment when Agamemnon enters with Cassandra, the single speaker has been far more explicator than tragic figure, and Agamemnon himself remains on the stage for less than one-tenth of the play. Of course, Aeschylus never used more than two speaking actors at one time: it was Sophocles' innovation to increase the number to three, which Euripides also kept to. In such circumstances we are a long way from the kind of tragedy that puts a particular man in a place of special eminence surrounded by lesser figures who contribute directly to the action – the kind that is most manifest in England in Marlowe's *Tamburlaine* or Shakespeare's *Hamlet*. If the Greeks wished to put a particular figure in a place of solitary eminence, they had to give him almost the whole of the non-choral part of the play, as Sophocles did for his Oedipus on two occasions. Even in recent times it is possible to find monologue dramas – Strindberg's *The Stronger* (1890), Jean Cocteau's *La Voix humaine* (1934), O'Neill's *Before Breakfast* (1916) – but such plays are short and without a chorus. On the other hand, from fifth-century Athens to the present day we have tragedies where we cannot firmly state that a particular character is the tragic hero. The *Agamemnon* is not properly a case in point. Agamemnon, being on the stage for only a few minutes, can hardly, though he is indeed here the victim, exercise the authority we need for a 'hero': this is, however, the first part of a firmly knit trilogy, acted on a single occasion, and the Orestes who is merely mentioned in the first play will bear the main role in the second and third, will in effect dominate the total performance. But *The Trojan Women* brings the matter fully before us. We cannot say that Hecuba or Andromache has prime place here: the very title of the play indicates a collective doom. Kitto, moreover, has drawn attention to the way in which Ajax dies some time before the end of the Sophocles play which uses his name as title (*Form and Meaning in Drama*, pp. 196 ff.). It is the *subject* of Ajax' madness and rebellion and death, he says, that constitutes the heart of the play, not the presentation of him as a sufferer: the play discusses his case rather than presents him as its essential and focal point. Even so, it is possible for us to think that the presence of Ajax the living man is still strongly felt even when the dispute about his burial is going on. In more recent times Shakespeare's *Julius Caesar* is at least as much about Brutus and Cassius and Antony as about Caesar; double titles are used for *Romeo and Juliet* and *Antony and Cleopatra*; Webster's Duchess of Malfi, like Shakespeare's Antony, dies at the end of Act IV. Although we may see that Antony and the Duchess preside over the fifth acts in which they are already dead, we have nevertheless to recognize that the total disaster encompasses those who die in the play's last phase. Aristotle, it may be admitted, puts too much stress on the type of structure where a single figure, such as Oedipus, dominates the whole action. We have to recognize that the tragic burden can be shared. In Marlowe's *Edward II* Mortimer has a tragic position as well as the King, though certainly there the stress is on Edward as in *The Duchess of Malfi* it is on the Duchess. Yet can we certainly say that in Webster's other major tragedy, *The White Devil*, it is Vittoria, not Flamineo, not in some places Brachiano, who demands our central regard? I have already implied a doubt whether we can fix that regard securely on Brutus in *Julius Caesar*.

The tragic hero – as Conrad said of Lord Jim in the preface to the novel where Jim was the focus of regard – is 'one of us'. He is not necessarily virtuous, not necessarily free from profound guilt. What he is is a man who reminds us strongly of our own humanity, who can be accepted as standing for us. But tragedies can be written in which the focus is shifting, as it frequently is in 'tragic novels' – as in *Nostromo*, for example, where Nostromo and Charles Gould and Gould's wife and Antonia and Decoud can share the tragic burden, implying indeed a universal demand on us to share it; as too in *The Trojan Women* and the *Antigone*, where Hecuba and Andromache and Antigone and Creon are in turn made the prime objects of our consideration.

4

Cleansing?
or Sacrifice?

Of all technical terms, *'catharsis'* is probably the one most often used in relation to tragedy. It first appears in this context in Aristotle's definition of the Kind, which has been quoted in Chapter 1. There is general agreement that it came into his picture through his wish to counter Plato's argument, given notable expression in Book X of *The Republic*, that the poets were to be blamed, and exiled, because their arousing of emotions, including that of pity, worked against a man's duty to follow the dictates of reason. Combating this, Aristotle asserted that the emotions, particularly those of pity and fear, in being aroused in tragedy, were also 'purged'. Taking his cue, apparently, from the use of music to quieten patients suffering from mental disturbance (as S. H. Butcher points out in *Aristotle's Theory of Poetry and Fine Art*, pp. 248–9), he argued that tragedy could, we may say, 'exorcise'. Whether he meant that the emotions of pity and fear were thus eliminated from the system, or that they were purged of the dross in them, has been a matter of controversy. The latter view seems half-acknowledged by Milton in the preface to *Samson Agonistes*, where tragedy, he declares, is

> said by *Aristotle* to be of power by raising pity and fear, or terror, to purge the mind of those and such like passions, that is to temper and reduce them to just measure with a kind of delight, stirr'd up by reading or seeing those passions well imitated.

He proceeds to illustrate from medical practice:

for so in Physic things of melancholic hue and quality are us'd against melancholy, sowr against sowr, salt to remove salt humours.

Thus he refers to the tempering of the emotions and the reducing of them 'to just measure', although his analogue from medicine would rather seem to imply elimination. Lessing in *Hamburgische Dramaturgie* (1769) argued that through the arousing of 'fear' for ourselves (for disaster might come upon us too) our 'pity' is rendered more acute, and we are consequently readier to respond to the distresses of our fellow men. This is 'enlightened', but seems a wrenching of Aristotle's words. Nevertheless, the idea that *catharsis* implies some kind of purification has been recurrent in literary theory since Lessing's time. Butcher suggested that in tragedy we experience pity and fear without the pain that is customarily associated with them because the action presented has a universal application: the tragic figures are beings like ourselves but with a greatness transcending our reach, with a demand on them to face disasters that are more extreme than ours: consequently, the pity and fear we customarily experience are brought into comparative insignificance. Humphry House, in his posthumously published book *Aristotle's Poetics* (1956), thought also of the directing of the emotional responses through tragedy:

> A tragedy rouses the emotions from potentiality to activity by worthy and adequate stimuli; it controls them by directing them to the right objects in the right way; and exercises them within the limits of the play as the emotions of the good man would be exercised. When they subside to potentiality again after the play is over it is a more 'trained' potentiality than before. This is what Aristotle calls κάθαρσις. Our responses are brought nearer to those of the good and wise man.
>
> (pp. 109–10)

We may agree that this is an effect of tragedy – for the moment we are better, more sensitive and enlightened people in witnessing tragedy than we commonly are – but we may wonder if Aristotle's words allow us to assume he meant *catharsis* in this way, and if this utterance is adequate for the complexity of the tragic impact.

Gerald F. Else suggests that both the idea of eliminating and the idea of purifying pity and fear are mistaken. In *Aristotle's Poetics: The Argument* (1957), he contends that Aristotle had in mind the purging of the tragic event. We cannot in 'real life' contemplate parricide or incest with any approach to equanimity, but in *Oedipus* we can see them as tolerable because of the special circumstances in which they are presented to us. Medea's killing of her children, Antigone's doom – we might add the blinding of Gloucester and the madness of Lear – would be overwhelming if we encountered them outside a theatre. Aristotle is presented as arguing that in a theatre all the remoteness and authority of dramatic production (or, in reading, the splendour of the poetry) give them the distance and compensation that allow us to observe them with equanimity. But, Else freely admits, this only dubiously works in Greek tragedy and perhaps not at all in later tragedy. We do not in fact preserve our equanimity in watching *Lear*. If Aristotle meant what Else suggests he meant, the Aristotelian notion of *catharsis* does not help us much. When Renaissance and post-Renaissance writers have had *catharsis* in mind, as Milton for example had, it was a *catharsis* of a different kind. Milton thought that the goodness of Samson's last deed (which of course we may be doubtful about, but Milton was not to know that) left us calm in our minds because we could rejoice even as we recognized, as he did, that there would come a time for mourning later: for a moment, if Milton's intended effect is realized, we feel that there has been a lifting of a burden, not a purifying of a deed.

Not surprisingly, there has been total scepticism on this matter. Lodovico Castelvetro in his *Commentary on Aristotle's Poetics* (1570) insisted that *catharsis* was merely incidental: what mattered was the 'delight' (Horace's '*dulce*' in his *Ars Poetica*) that all poetry should give. In recent times we have all occasionally felt, with F.

L. Lucas in his *Tragedy in relation to Aristotle's Poetics* (1927), that the term is commonly used as a mere gesture of reverence and has no connection with our actual experience of tragedy. This indeed is the substance of D. M. Hill's argument in his article '"Catharsis": An Excision from the Dictionary of Critical Terms' (*Essays in Criticism*, VIII (1958), 113–19). More recently it has been used as a term of abuse. When Peter Brook directed *Lear* for the Royal Shakespeare Theatre, he manipulated Shakespeare's play in order to have the audience leave the theatre 'shaken' but not 'assured': 'Our problem with *Lear*,' said Charles Marovitz, who worked with Brook on the production, 'is that like all great tragedies it produces a catharsis' ('*Lear* Log', *Encore*, X (1963), 22). So much the worse for *catharsis* and for those unhappy dramatists who induced it and have to be adapted so that *catharsis* itself can be eliminated. 'We want them to feel fear anyway' seems to have been the guiding line of this production.

Yet do we ever go away feeling fear? Do we go away feeling that any capacity for emotion has been taken away from us? I can remember a performance of *Lear* at Stratford-upon-Avon which I saw in company with a colleague. It was our custom to go for a walk in the night air after visiting the theatre, and I suggested we should do it on this occasion. 'Yes,' he said, 'a walk, but I don't want to talk.' He was right, of course, and we did not talk though we walked for a few miles in the night. It had been a more than worthy production of perhaps the world's greatest tragedy, with Gielgud as the king. We were not feeling free from emotion, we were not frightened, we had not been impelled to take up arms. Our condition was one of tension still, of feeling a need to re-orientate but with no specific programme suggested to us. 'This is how things are' is an inadequate way of suggesting the kind of cognition we experienced. Rather, 'this is what we have to face, and we do not know, and we cannot quarrel with the dramatist for not telling us, how to face it'. We dare not equate ourselves with

Lear: 'we that are young [or middle-aged or old]/Shall never see so much nor live so long.' But his death has been an emblem of our deaths, his madness of the frenzy that we too, from time to time, know, his rejection of Cordelia of the rejections that we have made. We are not frightened, because we have seen it all as part of a condition we are born to, as something involving a kind of splendour: that, indeed, should fortify us. But the fortifying is coexistent with the heightened state of recognition with which, at least for a brief time, we shall live. Perhaps not merely for a brief time: to encounter *Lear* fully is to have made a major advance in self-knowledge and in knowledge of the world.

In a sense, the king has suffered and died for us. The analogy with the idea of Christ's sacrifice is strong. The major scapegoat of the West, although in the New Testament his story is not told as a tragedy, can be seen in association with our tragic heroes, those from the Renaissance onwards as well as those the Greeks have given us. John Holloway's *The Story of the Night* (1961) has stressed the idea of the scapegoat in Shakespearian tragedy. In ancient days the King was seen as, when his time came, dying for the people: he took with him their sins. This is a substratum of the tragic idea that we have to bear in mind when Oedipus declares that the man must suffer who has brought the plague on Thebes and then discovers he has named himself. Sartre in *Les Mouches* shows Orestes as willingly accepting the guilt of Argos:

> *Orestes.* [*Drawing himself up to his full height.*] So here you are, my true and loyal subjects? I am Orestes, your King, son of Agamemnon, and this is my coronation day. [*Exclamations of amazement, mutterings amongst the crowd.*] Ah, you are lowering your tone? [*Complete silence.*] I know; you fear me. Fifteen years ago to the day, another murderer showed himself to you, his arms red to the elbows, gloved in blood. But him you did not fear; you read in his eyes that he was of your kind, he had not the courage of his crimes. A crime which its doer disowns becomes ownerless – no man's crime; that's how you see it, isn't it? More like an accident than a crime?

So you welcomed the criminal as your King, and that crime without an owner started prowling round the city, whimpering like a dog that has lost its master. You see me, men of Argos, you understand that my crime is wholly mine; I claim it as my own, for all to know, it is my glory, my life's work, and you can neither punish me nor pity me. That is why I fill you with fear.

And yet, my people, I love you, and it was for your sake that I killed. For your sake. I had come to claim my kingdom, and you would have none of me because I was not of your kind. Now, I am of your kind, my subjects; there is a bond of blood between us, and I have earned my kingship over you.

As for your sins and your remorse, your night-fears, and the crime Aegisthus committed – all are mine, I take them all upon me. Fear your Dead no longer; they are *my* Dead. And, see, your faithful flies have left you, and come to me. But have no fear, people of Argos. I shall not sit on my victim's throne or take the sceptre in my blood-stained hands. A god offered it to me, and I said 'No.' I wish to be a king without a kingdom, without subjects.

Farewell, my people. Try to reshape your lives. All here is new, all must begin anew. And for me, too, a new life is beginning. A strange life . . .

Listen now to this tale. One summer there was a plague of rats in Scyros. It was like a foul disease; they soiled and nibbled everything, and the people of the city were at their wits' end. But one day a flute-player came to the city. He took his stand in the market-place. Like this. [ORESTES *rises to his feet*.] He began playing on his flute and all the rats came out and crowded round him. Then he started off, taking long strides – like this. [*He comes down from the pedestal.*] And he called to the people of Scyros, 'Make way!' [*The* CROWD *makes way for him.*] And all the rats raised their heads and hesitated – as the flies are doing. Look! Look at the flies! Then all of a sudden they followed in his train. And the flute-player, with his rats, vanished for ever. Thus.

He strides out into the light. Shrieking, the FURIES *fling themselves after him.*

(*The Flies and In Camera*, translated by Stuart Gilbert, 1946, pp. 102–3)

But neither Sophocles' Oedipus nor Sartre's Orestes goes to death; Oedipus is not even allowed exile till long after the end of the play in which his guilt is brought home. The driving out, as distinct from the killing, of a scapegoat is firmly established as an alternative rite in primitive societies, yet in Sophocles' play Creon's insistence that Oedipus remain in Thebes, blind and in shame, seems a deliberate refusing to the audience of the kind of release that they are subconsciously seeking. In Sartre, Orestes wills his exile, his taking the Flies with him: his speech illustrates, in an unusually explicit fashion, that willing of, acceptance of, necessity that we saw in Chapter 3 as inherent in the idea of the tragic hero. It should be noted that Orestes claims that his crime is his own, yet he acknowledges that it has made him one with the people, that their crimes too are, in his act of acceptance, being taken on his head. Sophocles and Sartre offer here two variants on the scapegoat pattern, sharply remote from each other in time and in idea; together they make us conscious of the difference between the simple rite and what tragedy has to offer.

Yet, though below the level of immediate consciousness, we may sense that Hamlet and Lear die for us: they have taken our burden on them. If so, we have to ask if we can endure the thought that a man suffers and then dies for us. It was well enough for a primitive society such as Frazer described in *The Golden Bough* to think it could get rid of its sins by killing or driving out a man or an animal that had been saddled with them. It was understandable that a society where kingship was a potent idea should from time to time see the king's death as similarly exculpating: Mary Renault has vividly demonstrated this in her novels about Theseus, *The King must Die* (1958) and *The Bull from the Sea* (1962). But the situation was not so simple in Athens in the fifth century B.C., in seventeenth-century England or France, in the world we now live in. These have been, for all their shortcomings, highly self-conscious societies, with a strong sense of the individual's responsibility to himself. The individual in such times and places cannot so easily get rid of his guilt, yet has enough of the primitive in him to respond to the notion – again I emphasize below the level of immediate consciousness – that another man may take that guilt on him. The barely perceived response is accompanied by a bewildered resentment, both because expiation somehow seems demanded and because there is the feeling that a vicarious way out has been found. In rational terms, we know that no man's death purges us, but, in so far as we sense that a vicarious purging gives us relief, we rebel against it. For a moment we may accept the scapegoat-ritual, but in our hearts we feel shame at our acceptance. The ultimate effect of tragedy is to sharpen our feeling of responsibility, to make us more fully aware that we have erred as the tragic figures have erred (whether they be many or one in the play we see). We cry out against what has happened. We have experienced a *catharsis* only to reject it.

In Alejo Carpentier's novel *The Lost Steps* we have a description of a funeral ceremony performed by South American Indians, where the shaman cries out in his strife with the forces of death, but the crying is at once converted into an expression of lament and protest. Even in this simplest of rites we have a recognition that no outcry will drive death away:

> As it went on, this outcry over a corpse surrounded by silent dogs became horrible, terrifying. The shaman now stood facing the body, shouting, thumping his heels on the ground in the paroxysm of a fury of imprecation which held the basic elements of all tragedy – the earliest attempt to combat the forces of annihilation which frustrate man's designs. I tried to remain outside, to establish distances. And yet I could not resist the horrid fascination this ceremony held for me. . . .
>
> Before the stubbornness of Death, which refused to release its prey, the Word suddenly grew faint and disheartened. In the mouth of the shaman, the spell-working orifice, the *Threne* – for that was what this

was – gasped and died away convulsively, blinding me to the realization that I had just witnessed the Birth of Music.

(*The Lost Steps*, translated by Harriet de Onés, New York, 1956, pp. 184–5)

So the fifth-century Athenians, the seventeenth-century Londoners – like ourselves – knew that rites do not work according to their initial purpose. We dare not accept a scapegoat in our conscious minds, we dare not claim that tragedy purges us.

A thing that emerges from all this is the significance of tragedy as performance, as rite. In the quotations from John Hopkins and Bertrand Russell given in Chapter 1 we have expressions of the sense of relief (if relief it is) that tragedy presents what is past: because, as we have seen, we are made to feel that the tragic figures are doomed from the beginning, we the living audience are at once separated from them. The dead are with us, but we can do no more about them. 'It all happened a long way off and a long time ago,' said the legendary spectators of a village performance of *The Trojan Women*, 'and let us hope it never really happened at all.' We cannot say that about historical figures, nor could the Greeks about the men and women of legend whose past they had absorbed into their minds. Nor can we, securely, say it about any tragic figure whose authority has been exercised on us (like Othello, whose story was never more than fictional). But they are now dead. They are, in an important sense, beyond our reach and grasp. Even historical figures are merely historical. Che Guevara, so recent in our history, cannot be brought back: he is beginning to be taken as an *exemplum* in drama. But the notable thing is that any successful tragedy makes us feel simultaneously that we have done with the situation and that we are still desperately concerned with it. The matter must be considered further in the next section.

5
The Sense
of Balance

Aristotle never argued that pity and fear balanced one another.
That was for I. A. Richards to tell us in his *Principles of Literary
Criticism* (1924). If the force of the one exceeded that of the other,
he said, we should no longer have tragedy, and this made him
declare:

> It is the relation between the two sets of impulses, Pity and Terror,
> which gives its specific character to Tragedy, and from that relation
> the peculiar poise of the Tragic experience springs.

(p. 247)

He argued further that 'the greater part of Greek Tragedy as well
as almost all of Elizabethan Tragedy outside Shakespeare's six
masterpieces' is 'pseudo-tragedy': 'Parody easily overthrows it,
the ironic addition paralyses it; even a mediocre joke may make it
look lopsided and extravagant' (pp. 247–8). Tragedy, he says, gives
us 'Pity, the impulse to approach, and Terror, the impulse to
retreat' brought into 'a reconciliation which they find nowhere
else' (p. 245). It was possible for F. L. Lucas to ask whether an
overplus of Pity would drive us on to the stage, an overplus of
Terror outside the theatre (*Tragedy in relation to Aristotle's
Poetics*, p. 49). The comment was facetious but apposite. Pity is
exercised on behalf of the suffering characters, Terror in relation
to the doom that confronts them: it is difficult to imagine a pair of
scales that could weigh them one against the other. I have myself
argued that the true opposition is between Terror at the threat and

Pride in the greatness of the sufferer (*Shakespeare's Tragedies and Other Studies in Seventeenth Century Drama*, 1950, p. 16), and I do not wish to withdraw this although I no longer feel that the essence of tragedy lies there. 'Pride' seems now to be too simple a term for the dominant feeling that the tragic character gives rise to in us.

Moreover, Richards is hardly justified in implying, if he does (the point is obscure), that his balance of Pity and Terror is Aristotelian. Hegel's idea of balance – most notably between the claims of Creon and Antigone, which is his most famous example – is admittedly something new. We do have to recognize that tragedy is often concerned with 'mighty opposites', as Hamlet put it in speaking of himself and Claudius: Claudius, the *de facto* king, had a case as well as Hamlet, who had in his own view *de jure* rights. In Shakespeare's histories, which move towards the tragic idea without asserting it, we feel something of this balance between Henry VI and Richard of York, between Richard II and Bolingbroke, between Henry VIII and those many who encountered his wrath. Macbeth and Duncan, Antony and Octavius, Coriolanus and the Tribunes, represent valid points of view on each side. The disaster that emerges is due to the opposition.

Una Ellis-Fermor in *The Frontiers of Drama* (1945) has a chapter on 'The Equilibrium of Tragedy' in which she argues that a characteristic effect of tragedy is the sense of a balance between the view that the world is governed by an alien and hostile destiny and the view that somehow this apparent evil may be explained in terms of good. Here she is in tune with the concept that Bradley put before us in the words quoted here in Chapter 1. But in arguing that Aeschylus in the *Oresteia* makes us aware of a process working ultimately to good in his choruses, that Kent and Cordelia after all exist, she seems to offer an insufficient counterweight to the bloodshedding and mental distress. We might similarly argue that when Yeats and Synge presented the story of Deirdre their glorying in Ireland's great legend allowed their audiences to feel acquiescent in the girl's disaster. She was, after all, a magical figure in their nation's story, and they could take pride in her (and what she had bequeathed to them) while sharing her anguish. That does, in a sense, work, as Elizabethan Englishmen could respond to Henry V as 'this star of England' in the epilogue to *Henry V* while feeling sadness at his death. But we may be dubious whether this is what tragedy ultimately does to us.

Certainly it is a rite, a celebration of a past act. In that way it is distanced: as we saw in Chapter 4, we are, in a restricted sense, now safe from it. Certainly, also, it is about men we can recognize as sharing with us the human condition. The effect of balance is there obvious. Certainly it often concerns itself with opponents who can – at least in some measure – each claim right on his side. The anguish is thereby increased. But the effect is enhanced, in a way that Aristotle did not recognize, by the fact that it is presented to us in a theatre, with living actors (our contemporaries, ordinary men) impersonating dead figures (for the tragic character, we have seen, is doomed from the beginning) who are extraordinary in their speech and in the degree of their suffering (as commonly we are not). We have seen, too, that the sense of rite is juxtaposed with our sense that the action is immediately happening: even in the Greek theatre, with its high degree of formality, this must have been to some extent true. We may compare the at least equally formal Mass, where the bread and wine are felt on each occasion to become body and blood. Certainly it was true in the Elizabethan-Jacobean theatre where, as T. S. Eliot has pointed out in his essay on 'Four Elizabethan Dramatists' (*Selected Essays*, 1932, pp. 109–17), we have a mixed mode. Dramatists of our day use an apparent – in the best writers, only an apparent – informality of language, but any theatre-performance remains largely a rite, which we know is intended to be performed, has in most cases been performed, many times over. 'They are all dead now,' we say as we leave, but we know 'they' are going home to supper, and in another sense 'they' will re-enact the rite tomorrow.

When a man dies, he is always 'done with' as far as we are concerned. We can at last see him, we think, whole. It may be distressing, but we are in a position we perhaps did not anticipate, when he might still have surprised us. But a tragic figure is in a rather different position. We know all about him, as we cannot know all about a real-life being. What the dramatist does not tell us does not exist. In the nineteenth century it was possible for Mrs Anna Jameson to speak (surely illegitimately) about the girl-hood of Shakespeare's heroines, and all of us have wondered (have felt we have been invited to wonder) about what happened to this or that character after a comedy ended. But in tragedy there is no future for the dead hero, the dead subordinate figures, and their past exists only to the extent that we have been told about it. So we know all, as we are in no position to know about a man we have met. There may be difficulties of interpretation (outstanding with Hamlet), but the evidence is all securely in front of us: it is either our or the dramatist's fault, more often ours perhaps if the drama-tist is major, when we fall out about what sort of a man he was. 'Ite, missa est,' says the celebrant at Mass (or did, when the authority of Latin was not abandoned). We have it all before us as we never have in life. Yet it is in tragedy, above all literary Kinds, that we have felt most fully aware of the presence of living beings. The novel may be 'tragic', and is perhaps at its most splendid when it is; but the novel does not show us people manifestly of our kin acting out the story before our eyes. Swann embracing Odette de Crécy in the coach has to be a much more distant figure than an actor playing Hamlet rejecting an actress (or boy-actor) playing Ophelia, a man in the role of Othello smothering his Desdemona, a man as Lear carrying his Cordelia in his arms. That supreme paradox – the living actor playing the dead man, the ordinary person manifesting the unspeakable woe – is surely at the heart of our balance of emotion when we watch tragedy. But balance does not mean equanimity. Rather, it gives to our response its peculiar anguish, its basic sense of puzzlement.

6
Peripeteia, Anagnorisis, Suffering

In Chapter VI of *The Poetics* Aristotle is urging the prime importance of Plot among the constituent parts of tragedy, and one of his
arguments is that, in Bywater's words, 'the most powerful elements
of attraction in Tragedy, the Peripeties and Discoveries, are parts
of the Plot'. He proceeds to define these terms in Chapter XI.
Peripety

> is the change from one state of things within the play to its opposite
> of the kind described, and that too in the way we are saying, in the
> probable or necessary sequence of events; as it is for instance in
> *Oedipus*: here the opposite of things is produced by the Messenger,
> who, coming to gladden Oedipus and to remove his fears as to his
> mother, reveals the secret of his birth.

> (Bywater's translation)

It is not claimed by Aristotle that either Peripety or Discovery
('*anagnorisis*') is essential to tragedy: a change of fortune is necessarily involved, but Peripety is a sudden reversal which comes with
the effect of shock. Bywater (p. 199) mentions the views of
Johannes Vahlen in his edition of *The Poetics* (1866) and Walter
Lock (*Classical Review*, IX (1895), 251–3) that Peripety refers to
what happens when 'a man's actions . . . are found to have conse-
quences the direct opposite of what the agent meant or expected'.
This, of course, would fit very well the *Oedipus* example that
Aristotle gives, but Bywater points out that he proceeds to give
another example from the lost play *Lynceus* of Theodectes: here
the change is from bad fortune to good and has no relation to the

agent's intention. Lynceus being suddenly saved from execution. He would doubtless have accepted the saving of Orestes in *Iphigenia in Tauris* as equally an instance of Peripety. Nevertheless, Bywater's interpretation has not been accepted by all recent commentators. F. L. Lucas followed Vahlen in an article in *The Classical Review* (XXXVII (1923), 98–104), and in his *Tragedy in relation to Aristotle's Poetics*, where he puts the matter thus:

> For it is the perpetual tragic irony of the Tragedy of Life that again and again men do thus laboriously contrive their own annihilation, or kill the thing they love. When Dejanira, sending her husband the love-philtre which was to win him back, poisons him so that he dies cursing her; when Oedipus runs headlong into the jaws of the very destiny from which he is fleeing; when Barabas falls into his own boiling cauldron; when Othello at last sees himself as one who has flung away like an ignorant savage the priceless jewel of his happiness; when Macbeth is lured by the equivocations of the devil to make his own perdition sure; when Lear delivers himself into the hands of the two daughters that despise him and torments the only one that loves – all these are *peripeteias* in the true sense of Aristotle. For the most poignant tragedy of human life is the work of human blindness – the Tragedy of Errors.
>
> (p. 93)

This, in the Shakespeare examples cited, quite overlooks the idea of suddenness that is surely implicit in Aristotle's words. Yet more recently Humphry House took the same line in *Aristotle's Poetics* (1956):

> In the word peripety is contained the idea of the boomerang or recoil effect of one's own actions, of being hoist with one's own petard, falling into the pit that one has dug for someone else. The action is complex because it moves on two levels, as it appears to the doer and as it really is, and because the cause of the disaster is woven in with the good intentions and right means to achieve them.
>
> (p. 97)

House supports this by referring to various uses of the term *peripeteia* from Homer onwards.

What Aristotle meant is for Greek scholars to argue over. D. W. Lucas, *Aristotle: Poetics* (Oxford, 1968), has said: 'Certainly if A. did mean to confine it to cases of reversed intention, his language is inept.' What we can say is that *peripeteia*, in the sense that Vahlen, Lock, F. L. Lucas and House and others take it, will not work often for modern tragedy. (Aristotle, of course acknowledged that his *peripeteia* was not essential but only valuable in achieving the tragic effect.) Macbeth 'falls', but he knows well enough from the start that his killing of Duncan is a dangerous act, and long before the play's ending he is aware of the uselessness of the kingship he has won. Hamlet is aware of a 'cursed spite' from the end of the first act. We could say that Lear and Othello acted so as to gain peace and found its opposite, that Faustus wanted power and found himself powerless in the most important things. But the concept will not work at all with Tamburlaine, with the Duchess of Malfi (who knows she is going into a 'wilderness' when she marries Antonio), with Danton in Büchner's *Danton's Death* (who knows how dangerously he is living), with the man and woman in Lorca's *Blood Wedding* who affront their society's ways, or with Strindberg's Julie, with Arthur Miller's Eddie Carbone (who is desperate from the start), with Rosencrantz and Guildenstern in Stoppard's play (for they do nothing, are only acted upon). The kind of irony Lucas speaks of can be seen in McGrath's *Events while guarding the Bofors Gun*, where Lance-Bombardier Evans does, he thinks, everything possible to realize the promise of officer-status and a trip to England and, because he does so, will after the play's end find himself for a long while in an army prison. However, all who have discussed the matter are, it appears, in agreement (1) that a change of fortune is basic in tragedy, (2) that a sudden change is likely to have a greater impact, and (3) that *peripeteia* as interpreted by Vahlen is a special effect of marked ironic force.

Anagnorisis is another matter, and it seems legitimate to argue that it is essential. Aristotle's definition is simple:

> A Discovery is, as the very word implies, a change from ignorance to knowledge, and thus to either love or hate, in the personages marked for good or evil fortune. (Bywater's translation)

The mention of 'to either love or hate' is curious here, for he adds that the discovery may be of 'things of a very casual kind' where the qualifying phrase does not seem appropriate. Such a 'casual' discovery might be exemplified in Hamlet's realization that the skull he holds is Yorick's. However, it is evident that what is primarily involved in the use of the term is something crucial to the plot, and, if we take away the notion of suddenness that Aristotle seems to imply, we may go so far as to claim that this – not *catharsis* as an ultimate effect, not *hamartia* – comes as near as we can get to the essence of tragedy. In discussing this, let us first take the least favourable example, *The Trojan Women*. Before the play begins, Troy has fallen, the men are dead; the women now wait to be disposed of. But so long as we are alive we do not know all yet. Andromache has still to experience what it feels like to have Astyanax taken from her and given to death. No one among them knows exactly how it will be when they are led away into subjection and concubinage. The ultimate irony in human life is that there is still, while it goes on, something further to know: in tragedy the as yet unimagined becomes real. Macbeth, as we have seen, knows how dangerous his initial evil act is, but as the play progresses he makes ever fresh discoveries of how it feels to be gone so far in evil that 'Returning were as tedious as go o'er'. Tamburlaine only ultimately realizes that even the Scourge of God must die; Faustus anticipates damnation some while before his end, but he does not, cannot, know what his last hour will be like until the experience comes upon him. Rosencrantz and Guildenstern in Stoppard's play, however much their fear grows during the course of the action, cannot see in advance Hamlet's alteration of the letter they are carrying. The lovers in Flecker's *Hassan*, when they appear as ghosts, acknowledge their choice was wrong (as the man half-knew, but only half-knew, before): the idea of 'protracted death' can be put aside during a first night of love, but its realization is a totally different matter.

To see things plain – that is *anagnorisis*, and it is the ultimate experience we shall have if we have leisure at the point of death (or its near-equivalent, as for Adolph in Strindberg's *The Father*, for Hecuba and Andromache in *The Trojan Women*, for Mrs Alving in Ibsen's *Ghosts*). It does not matter whether we have been 'great' before. Marlowe's Edward II, we have seen, was a poor thing, a fumbling man. When the spit entered him, he knew he had reached his goal. When Byron in Chapman's *The Conspiracy and Tragedy of Charles Duke of Byron* (1608) found that, despite his previous incredulity, he had to bow his head before the axe, this too was *anagnorisis*. Like Büchner's *Danton's Death*, Chapman's play is especially remarkable in drawing our attention to the difficulty we have in envisaging our own death. Even if we have reason to know, either for physiological reasons or because we are engaged in especially dangerous pursuits (as in war), that any day may bring death to us, we still cannot live it through in advance. When first its certainty and then its moment of realization come to us, we have the sudden confrontation with the end. That is, for all of us (unless, perhaps, we can die so quickly as not to know of it), the supreme *anagnorisis*. It is what tragedy ultimately is about: the realization of the unthinkable. An approach to it must be when the doors close on us in a prison or a mental hospital: we may get out from either, but the unthinkable has nevertheless happened. We may indeed fear death less than incarceration of one sort or another (or chronic invalidism), yet the sense of the final experience has its special acuteness: it is, after all, the last moment of consciousness. For that reason the *Oedipus at Colonus* has, it may be, a fuller tragic impact than ever the *Oedipus the King*. Edmund Wilson asks us to consider again the later play:

> Did one find even in the Oedipus of Colonus that spirit of peace and resignation with which Victorian critics sometimes credited it? Was the exiled and embittered king a figure of mellow clemency? Surely his final cursing of his sons was one of the most shocking scenes in literature! – nor did the species of divine electrocution with which Sophocles finally disposed of him strike precisely a note of tranquillity.
>
> (*I Thought of Daisy*, London, n.d.,
> pp. 156–7)

In another novel, *The Bull from the Sea*, – and we often owe to the novelists the most sensitive exploration of the high and dreadful moments of tragedy – Mary Renault has retold the ending of Oedipus' life. She shows Oedipus looking back over the range of his experience, knowing that he has found the place and time of its ending, recognizing that no man is at all levels of consciousness free from guilt, suggesting that he and Jocasta had closed their minds to what, deep down, they knew. Lear has a moment of supreme *anagnorisis* when he enters carrying the dead Cordelia, though, in a subtle variant on the usual pattern, he tries to talk himself out of it right up to his last moment. In *Events while guarding the Bofors Gun*, Evans has his moment too (it was not yet death for him, but bad enough) when he heard Sergeant Walker say: 'You won't be going home, you know. Not for donkey's years.'

It was highly appropriate that, in the same chapter as that in which he talked of *peripeteia* and *anagnorisis*, Aristotle added:

> A third part is Suffering; which we may define as an action of a destructive or painful nature, such as murders on the stage, tortures, woundings, and the like.
>
> (Bywater's translation)

Of course, Aristotle does not mean that murders or other deeds of violence were shown on the stage: rather, the action is about such things. We may say indeed that tragedy is about 'suffering' (*pathos*) leading to *anagnorisis*. We must not take Aristotle's *pathos* as equivalent to the 'pathetic', a term we have come to use for a relaxed response to people's suffering, generally transient, held only pleasurably in the memory when a god or other power makes all well. The 'suffering' presented in tragedy is an image of something we intellectually know is in store for ourselves but cannot in imagination properly anticipate. The vigorous, the for-a-time 'successful', the self-confident revolutionary put it out of their minds, and this for the moment closes tragedy to them. But John Marston, though in many ways a minor dramatist, knew better. Only those, he saw, who have come to some understanding of the nature of suffering can properly respond to tragedy. In the passage from the prologue to *Antonio's Revenge* partly quoted in Chapter 1, he tells us that the performance is being given in winter (an image of death) and that he will give us a wintry vision of how men ultimately suffer: if we have not come to some realization of what that means, the spectacle will mean nothing to us; if we have reached such a realization, he is telling us about things we are in a position to respond to. This play came at the beginning of the time when Jacobean tragedy achieved its line of triumphs. As I have noted elsewhere (*Shakespeare's Tragedies and Other Studies*, pp. 29–31), the prologue is appropriate not only for Marston's horrific play but for the greater things that followed – the tragedies of Shakespeare and Webster and Chapman and Middleton and Ford.

Anagnorisis implies 'suffering': it is the agency through which suffering, in the ultimate, mental sense, is brought into full being. Aristotle's notion of *anagnorisis* is narrower than the one implied here, being restricted to those tragedies with 'complex plots': we have seen that he regarded *The Trojan Women* as being free from it. So, too, the *pathos* of tragedy need not involve the physical violence he mentions: Racine seems altogether justified in the passage from the preface to *Bérénice* quoted in Chapter 1. We may say that comedy can have its *anagnorisis* too, when the foolish recognize their folly, but they do not achieve this regularly in comedy (or only in the mild way of Phebe in *As You Like It*, of Orsino in *Twelfth Night*): their 'suffering' is, moreover, a passing thing. The final *anagnorisis* in tragedy has a sense of totality and gives us an image of what lies in wait for us on every day until our last.

Of course, tragedy is a form of writing, not of living. It would be absurd to suggest that for every human being the ultimate realization comes: death may interrupt things too quickly, or there may be refuges and subterfuges (into incredulity, into insanity, into resigning oneself to a divine power). Moreover, some degree of realization is a recurrent experience in human life (such as the *anagnorisis* of comedy represents): Saul became Paul through a journey to Damascus, and without that high degree of change we frequently recognize in our own lives that, because a particular event contributed in a major way to the pattern of our lives up to that point, nothing has been the same again. But tragedy is concerned with the dramatic presentation of an ending, the kind of ending that Sartre tells us about in his picture of Matthieu's last moments in *Les Chemins de la liberté*. When a writer shows us a man saying 'This is the end, this is how it feels, this is how life feels in relation to it', there we have the basic material of tragedy. We do not demand 'greatness' in the hero; if we feel 'purged', we resent the fact (as we saw in Chapter 4); but we do demand that the tragic figure or figures shall sense a point of no return. Andromache going into exile, Strindberg's Adolph to the asylum, countless others to death, Lance-Bombardier Evans to prison, Stanley in Pinter's *The Birthday Party* into Monty's care – these have the moment of *anagnorisis* not to be recovered from. Whether death or not, it is an image of what death, to a man aware, must be like.

John Gassner has put it in this way: 'Only enlightenment can therefore round out the esthetic experience in tragedy, can actually ensure complete esthetic gratification' ('Catharsis and the Modern Theater', in *Aristotle's 'Poetics' and English Literature: A Collection of Critical Essays*, edited by Elder Olson, Chicago and Toronto, 1965, p. 111). There is probably something too relaxed in the use of 'round out' and 'esthetic' and 'gratification' here, and Gassner too easily, I think, links the enlightenment with 'purgation' and with 'equilibrium'. Nevertheless, 'enlightenment' is properly climactic in this account of the tragic effect. It is tragedy's basic, and minimal, affirmation – an affirmation all the more valuable when, as in the passage quoted from Henry James in Chapter 1, the recognition is most painfully and most humiliatingly achieved.

7
The Chorus
and the Unities

No one can now insist on either Chorus or Unities, but a consideration of tragedy through the ages cannot neglect them. In the Greek theatre we may say that, in normal practice (though not in the *Eumenides*), the one required the other. After an introductory speech it was customary for the Chorus to enter and then to remain until, or almost until, the end. That established location and it also suggested a duration of time. All that Aristotle said, in Chapter V of *The Poetics*, was that 'Tragedy endeavours to keep as far as possible within a single circuit of the sun, or something near that'. We have seen above that the Chorus was historically, it appears, the first element in tragedy, then first one actor, then two (in Aeschylus), then three (in Sophocles), shared the performance with the Chorus, and that out of this development came the actual (as, doubtless, distinct from the referred to) central figure. For Aeschylus, the Chorus was responsible for something like half of the play's words; for Sophocles and Euripides much less. When Seneca in Rome wrote his tragedies for recitation before a small group, the choric passages had become only gnomic interludes between the acts. This was, too, the practice in Sackville and Norton's *Gorboduc* and in the other Inns of Court plays that followed in England, but Fulke Greville in his closet-play *Mustapha* could imagine a chorus in the old sense. When the term 'chorus' was used in the public theatre of that time, it was a label for a single anonymous speaker, the author's spokesman, as in *Romeo and Juliet* and *Henry V*, or, with a degree of ambiguity, the spokesman for a generalized comment that the audience would be expected to share, as in Marlowe's *Faustus*.

The ancient view of the Chorus's function is well summarized in Horace's *Ars Poetica*:

> The Chorus must back the good and give sage counsel; must control the passionate and cherish those that fear to do evil; it must praise the thrifty meal, the blessings of justice, the laws, and Peace with her unbarred gates. It will respect confidences and implore heaven that prosperity may revisit the miserable and quit the proud.
>
> (*Horace on the Art of Poetry*, edited by Edward Henry Blakeney, 1928, p. 49)

This presents the Chorus as voicing the wisdom that the audience, when it remembers, already has. This makes it, as has commonly been said, a group-representation of the audience and its memories, its fears, its aspirations. Not that it is not capable of special insight, when the dramatist expresses through its words those things that are hard to endure or gives to it a realization, beyond what the characters themselves have, of the oncoming march of events. So it is in the *Agamemnon*, where we are told by the Chorus that 'Against one's will comes wisdom;/The grace of the gods is forced on us/Throned inviolably' (translated by Louis MacNeice, reprinted 1937, p. 19), or when in *Oedipus the King* the Chorus is in advance of the king in seeing the coming of disaster. But the Chorus is made up of people, like the Women of Canterbury in *Murder in the Cathedral*, who want to live quietly:

> I only ask to live, with pure faith keeping
> In word and deed that Law which leaps the sky,
> Made of no mortal mould, undimmed, unsleeping
> Whose living godhead does not age or die.
>
> (*The Theban Plays*, translated by E. F. Watling, Harmondsworth, 1947, p. 52)

> We do not wish anything to happen.
> Seven years we have lived quietly,
> Succeeded in avoiding notice,
> Living and partly living.
> There have been oppression and luxury,
> There have been poverty and licence,
> There has been minor injustice.
> Yet we have gone on living,
> Living and partly living.
>
> (*Murder in the Cathedral*,
> reprinted 1940, pp. 18–19)

So they are in a sense representatives of the audience, except that the audience has come to watch a tragedy, the Chorus is fearful that a tragedy will take place in its immediate presence. When the Chorus became reduced to a single depersonalized speaker, it was generally, we have seen, a vehicle for the dramatist's own voice: this brought tragedy nearer to the epic manner, which Aristotle pointed out was characterized by an alternation of the poet speaking in his own person and the imagined characters speaking for themselves. For this reason, I think, the supreme tragedies of the seventeenth century, both in England and in France, abandoned the Chorus proper: neither Shakespeare in his major tragic work nor his English contemporaries and successors nor Racine in *Phèdre* and the other plays by him that we find most securely tragic utilized this mode of direct communication. They did not want the sense of distancing that the use of interpolated comment necessarily entailed.

Modern dramatists have on occasion returned to it. Yeats could not resist this Greek device, wanting as he did to give to Ireland a drama of Greek authority: the opening dialogue of the Sailors in *The Shadowy Waters* (1911) and that of the Musicians in *Deirdre* (1907) are essentially choric in function. O'Neill in *Mourning Becomes Electra*, based as we have seen on the *Oresteia*, has a Chorus of townsfolk who come to see and crassly comment on the

Mannon house, which is the main place of action, and on the family which the action directly concerns. We have already noted Eliot's use of a Chorus in *Murder in the Cathedral*: in his later plays he whittled this away, introducing a few choric speeches spoken by some of the named characters in *The Family Reunion* (1939), reducing this further to the speeches of the 'Guardians' when they are alone in *The Cocktail Party* (1950), and abandoning the device entirely thereafter. This development in Eliot was in line with his stated belief in his lecture *Poetry and Drama* (1951, reprinted in *On Poetry and Poets*, 1957) that it was best if the audience was not aware that what they were witnessing was tragedy in verse. The difficulty is that, unless the Chorus has the authority which music and choreographic movement gave to it in Greek tragedy, it becomes either a direct preachment from the dramatist (distancing the action in such a way that we are not likely to feel deeply involved in the disaster and the accompanying *anagnorisis*) or an altogether too commonplace group of speakers, as in *Mourning Becomes Electra*, for us to accept them as capable of sharing our degree of perception.

In most tragedies from the Renaissance onwards, whether or not – as in *Romeo and Juliet* and *Faustus* – they have a nominal 'Chorus', the true function of the old Chorus is discharged by the characters who surround the tragic figure. Sometimes there is a particular commentator among these characters – Horatio perhaps, Enobarbus certainly. In nineteenth-century English and French drama there was the 'raisonneur', who provided the voice of wisdom or commonsense which the principal characters disregarded at their peril. Usually, however, this was in plays that we can barely accept as tragic: either his advice was heeded in time, or the sad ending was, like that in Pinero's *The Second Mrs Tanqueray* (1893), a 'happy relief' for all concerned. More often we can feel that all those characters in a tragedy who escape disaster can be seen as a group comparable with the ancient Chorus. Bradley pointed out that the special stress on Macbeth and his wife made their particular tragedy in that respect closer than was usual to the ancient model (*Shakespearean Tragedy*, pp. 389–90). At its end, each of Shakespeare's major tragedies has something of a choric effect – in *Hamlet*, where Horatio and Fortinbras survive to speak appropriate words; in *Lear*, where the last lines are for Albany, Kent and Edgar, voicing their and our feeling of lamentation and incredulity; in *Othello*, when Lodovico and Cassio, performing a similar function, are nevertheless confronted with the still living figure of Iago (as the Chorus in the *Agamemnon* faced an Aegisthus as yet merely threatened by Orestes' return). So in *A View from the Bridge* Arthur Miller has used his lawyer Alfieri (an Italian immigrant to the United States, like the play's central figure) to voice final words of lament. The dramatist seems to need very often these figures who show the point of view of ordinary but percipient men, awed, horrified, as an intermediary between the tragic figure and ourselves. But they are not essential in modern tragedy. The tragic writer can let his figures' anguish speak for itself. Lorca in *The House of Bernarda Alba* has made the whole household into a kind of Chorus, but it is their tragedy too.

The Unities, we have seen, grew out of the presence of the Chorus through the play. The Renaissance writers Scaliger and Castelvetro deduced from Aristotle's comment on the customary limitation of time and from the practice of the Greek theatre that a single place (or perhaps town) should be used through the action, and that the duration should be limited to a single day or to the time of representation. This was a powerful influence on Renaissance writing. In no tragedy did Shakespeare fully accept the requirement (though he kept almost to a single place in *Hamlet* and, apart from Act I, to a single place and an ambiguously limited time in *Othello*), but in comedy he several times observed it (*Love's Labour's Lost*, *The Comedy of Errors*, *The Tempest*) in relation to both time and place, and he kept to a single place in

The Merry Wives of Windsor. No one can now demand this, but some writers have seen the practical advantages to be gained from it – Ibsen most notably, Strindberg not infrequently, Chekhov in relation to place though not to time, many film-makers of our day. Eliot has declared of the Unities:

> The laws (*not* rules) of unity of place and time remain valid in that every play which observes them *in so far as its material allows* is in that respect and degree superior to plays which observe them less. I believe that in every play in which they are not observed we only put up with their violation because we feel that something is gained which we could not have if the law *were* observed.
>
> (*The Use of Poetry and the Use of Criticism,* reprinted 1937, p. 45)

The way the Unities operate has been demonstrated in an extreme form in Sartre's *Huis Clos* (1944), and is given incidental illustration in Roger Vailland's novel *A Young Trout*:

> It is fascinating to observe, within the strictly defined boundaries of a fish-tank (comparable with a boxing-ring or with the framework of a tragedy respectful of the three unities) the trial of strength which is displayed moment after moment in unequivocal actions and movements of blinding clarity, amid a violence which coerces living forms into wonderfully precise and elegant self-expression.
>
> (Translated by Peter Wiles, 1965, p. 72)

If the so-called Unities of Time and Place are observed, we feel more easily that the characters presented in the drama cannot get away from each other: they have to fight (and die sometimes); there is no room for anything but elegance or at least economy, no room to sprawl.

Not surprisingly, therefore, modern tragedy does often adhere to the Renaissance Unities, although we no longer believe in them as 'rules'. The Greeks, generally forced into them by the almost continuous presence of the Chorus, had thus a ready means of concentrating the attention, of making us feel the imminence of disaster, of the point of *anagnorisis*. So in later times Ibsen and Strindberg frequently kept to them, letting the long past manifest itself through exposition. The twentieth-century plays that come closest to tragedy (as Beckett's *Waiting for Godot*, Pinter's *The Caretaker*, McGrath's *Events while guarding the Bofors Gun*) have commonly restricted time and place to a minimum, though not necessarily restricting the action to a single day. We feel the *anagnorisis* more sharply if it manifestly lies in wait for the characters from the moment when we first behold them.

8
The Sense
of overdoing it

Here, finally, we touch on the aspect of tragedy that sets up adverse reactions, that makes some people feel that comedy is the more mature form. We have, I believe, every reason in fact to see comedy as a way out, as a Kind which excludes not only the ultimate anguish but the ultimate achievement of man. But the argument is understandable. The tragic hero makes a fuss. In Chapter 1 the quotation from *Lust's Dominion* is damaging: tragedy is to 'jet upon' the stage there, though we have to remember that this is a poor play. Stoppard's *Rosencrantz and Guildenstern are Dead* suggests that we should put Hamlet in his place, directing our sympathy towards the attendant lords who were to conduct him to death but found that their own deaths were to come prior to his and were to be less splendidly acclaimed. But their fate, too, was tragic, because they came to a realization of what was happening to them.

It is commonly urged that today we have not faith enough in man to see him as a tragic figure. Malraux, speaking through his young Chinese visiting Europe in *The Temptation of the West*, has put it to western man that

> For you, absolute reality was first God, then Man; but *Man is dead*, following God, and you search with anguish for something to which you can entrust his strange heritage. (Translated by Robert Hollander, New York, 1961, pp. 97–8)

This is the common view of writing tragedy today. To make our spokesman, the tragic hero, speak grandly is to defy the limits of our belief: all men are ordinary now. Yet this is no new idea. Horace in the *Ars Poetica* recognized that tragic heroes need to be brought close to us through the occasional ordinariness of their language:

> At times, however, even Comedy exalts her voice, and an angry Chremes rants and raves; often, too, in a tragedy Telephus or Peleus utters his sorrow in the language of prose, when, poor and in exile, he flings aside his paint-pots and his words a yard long, in eagerness to touch the spectator's heart with his lamentable tale. (Blakeney's translation, pp. 44–5.)

So Hamlet speaks casually to Rosencrantz and Guildenstern, to Horatio too at times, and thus makes us feel he is wholly one with us. Writers of recent years have generally abandoned verse for prose, have made their central figures (whom, as we have seen, they have hesitated to call 'tragic') as close to us as the theatre allows, in their diction and their status. Always the question arises, 'Do we dare claim tragic status for anyone?'

The novelists have not always been so modest. Hardy implied an echo of Greek tragedy in *Tess*, of the *Book of Job* in *Jude the Obscure*, Conrad and Melville (though Melville with an occasional hint of embarrassment, showing itself in a semi-facetious mode of utterance, in *Moby Dick*, and with the help that the concentrated short-fiction form gave him in *Billy Budd*) have left us with a sense that their central figures are as tragic as any person in imaginative literature can be. Murray Krieger in *The Tragic Vision* (reprinted Chicago, 1966) has indeed argued that true tragedy in our time is to be found only in the novel, because the formality of drama inhibits our full sense of disaster, and has – surely doubtfully – declared that the 'formlessness' of the novel gives us a properer sense of man totally face-to-face with the cosmos. We may well be unconvinced by this, because the tragic novel in its most manifest form (as in *Nostromo*, *Under the Volcano*, for example) has shown a formal organization surely comparable with that of any drama.

Yet one can glimpse what he means: the modern sense of the 'tragic' involves an increasing abandonment of the overt intention to write with tragic pomp. This, however, shows itself in some measure as early as *Hamlet*.

This tendency has had its effect even on the critical evaluation of dramas of the past. Wilbur Sanders, who has no special care for Marlowe, has objected to 'an air of contrivance' in

> Fair nature's eye, rise, rise again, and make
> Perpetual day; or let this hour be but
> A year, a month, a week, a natural day . . .

> (*Faustus*, xix, 138–40)

He asks: 'To put it as sharply as possible: do we *need* the repeated "rise"? would it matter if the "month" or the "week" were omitted?' (*The Dramatist and the Received Idea*, p. 240). He goes on to find Faustus' 'unmodulated key-changes' altogether 'too violent and too hectic': 'The poet seems to be himself in a state of near-delirium.' This is what happens when a man of the twentieth century, brought up in England's Cambridge, forces himself to contemplate the free rhetoric, the dwelling on the anguish, of the Elizabethans. A page earlier, Sanders suggests that Faustus' quotation from Ovid ('*O lente lente currite noctis equi!*') may be 'an obtrusion of a somewhat pedantic Marlowe when all attention should be focused on Faustus'. This, however, is to fail to see the devastating irony that should be found in the protagonist's lying with Helen as being the nearest approach to the beatific vision that he was ever to achieve: that Ovid asked for a longer night of love is wholly appropriate for Faustus to quote as he strains for a more extended day. But we can still understand why the critic has held back from sympathy. Should any dramatist make a character so explicit in his utterance? He has a right to do that, but he embarrasses many people today in doing so. Not surprisingly, dramatists of today are timid of the frontal attack, the blatant assertion, the great claim: they show a more oblique approach to the tragic.

To come on to a stage – and there to kiss, to betray, to kill, to die – is in some ways an outrage on us. In the plays of the last few years from which I have chosen to illustrate a continuing tragic effect (Harold Pinter's, Tom Stoppard's, John McGrath's – there are, of course, a considerable number of others that could have been mentioned) there is a deliberate withholding from the decisive action. The characters hesitate and debate, they do not do much. That is our way, in the world we live in, where so much is done to us and the only way we can exert ourselves is through doubtless ineffective speech. When violence occurs, as in *The Birthday Party* and in Edward Bond's *Saved* (1965), it seems pointless and arbitrary. So we do not, except in revivals of the classics, normally welcome a stage for tragedy to 'jet upon'. Peter Shaffer's *The Royal Hunt of the Sun* (1964) was a startling exception, which left some of its audience uncomfortable. Even in the Elizabethan years it appears that there was a sense of overdoing it if tragedy were too obtrusive and monotoned. Hence Shakespeare's mixed kind of writing, followed by Webster and Tourneur and Middleton. These dramatists felt as we feel – that, as far as the nature of the theatre of the time allows (and no theatre of any time can allow it wholly), the men and women of the stage must behave and speak as we do, suffer in a way that is not so different from ours, experience the kind of *anagnorisis* that we experience from time to time and that, in its ultimate form, we expect in the moment of death. In George Steiner's *The Death of Tragedy* (1961), the concluding pages suggest that tragedy has died to be reborn – in, for example, the silent scream of Mother Courage in Brecht's play. That is tragedy for us now, as Pinter also shows it in the over-talkative Davies coming to a final silence in *The Caretaker* (1960).

We have today tragedy for a minority audience, not for the whole city as in Athens, not for a large community as in early seventeenth-century England or in France a little later. Since the nineteenth century, when Kleist and Büchner led the way for Ibsen and Strindberg and their followers, since the time when Chekhov at the Moscow Art Theatre showed how tragedy could underlie what proclaimed itself to be comedy, we have had a tragedy that exists for those few who stand apart from the drugged world, who do not hold a blank banner aloft but respond to the dramatists and the novelists who remind us of the thing we shall finally know, the last *anagnorisis*, but do it quietly, letting the end come in one of Pinter's silences, in Conrad's despairing glance into the future in *Nostromo*, in the Consul's seemingly adventitious yet appropriate death in *Under the Volcano*, in the dumb marking-time of Lance-Bombardier Evans in *Events while guarding the Bofors Gun*. In such cases there is no overdoing it. We dare not make a last noise in this time when empty voices clamour round us. But never, surely, has there been a fuller sense of the tragic end.

Select Bibliography

A very great number of tragedies and their authors have been briefly commented on in ALLARDYCE NICOLL'S *World Drama* (1949), an indispensable reading-guide and reference book.

GREEK AND ROMAN TRAGEDY AND CRITICISM

The standard translation of ARISTOTLE'S *The Poetics* is still that by Ingram Bywater (Oxford, 1909). S. H. BUTCHER'S *Aristotle's Theory of Poetry and Fine Art* (1894) includes a translation and provides a searching and stimulating discussion of Aristotle's views. The introduction, commentary and appendices to D. W. Lucas's edition (Oxford, 1968) are of major importance. H. D. F. KITTO'S *Greek Tragedy: A Literary Study* (1939) gives an authoritative account of the plays, and his *Form and Meaning in Drama* (1956) discusses the *Oresteia* along with three plays of Sophocles and *Hamlet*. HUMPHRY HOUSE'S *Aristotle's Poetics* (1956) is a posthumous publication of lectures addressed to students of English at Oxford. F. L. LUCAS'S *Tragedy in relation to Aristotle's Poetics* (1928) considers Aristotle's ideas with wide reference to later drama. JOHN JONES'S *On Aristotle and Greek Tragedy* (1962) relates Aristotle to the three Greek tragic writers. WILLIAM CHASE GREENE'S *Moira: Fate, Good, and Evil in Greek Thought* (Cambridge, Massachusetts, 1944) devotes four of its eleven chapters to tragedy, and deals with a matter of major concern in any discussion of the Kind. ELDER OLSON'S *Aristotle's Poetics and English Literature* (Chicago and Toronto, 1965) is an anthology of critical essays, mainly American and twentieth-century, on the interpretation of Aristotle.

The translation of HORACE'S *Ars Poetica* used in this book is that of Edward Henry Blakeney (1928), which includes the Latin text.

On Seneca, the most informative account is F. L. LUCAS'S *Seneca and Elizabethan Tragedy* (1922). T. S. ELIOT wrote an introduction to the Tudor Translations edition of Seneca's plays (1927, reprinted in *Selected Essays*, 1932); his famous essay 'Shakespeare and the Stoicism of Seneca' (written from a standpoint rather unsympathetic with both Seneca and Shakespeare, but none the less important) was also included in *Selected Essays*. *Roman Drama*, edited by T. A. DOREY and DONALD R. DUDLEY (1965), includes essays by Gareth Lloyd-Evans on 'Shakespeare, Seneca, and the Kingdom of Violence' and by André Steegman on 'Seneca and Corneille'.

TRAGEDY FROM THE RENAISSANCE ONWARDS

J. M. R. MARGESON'S *The Origins of Elizabethan Tragedy* (Oxford, 1967) traces the emergence of tragedy from medieval and early sixteenth-century drama. Works on Shakespearian tragedy have, of course, been legion. A. C. BRADLEY'S *Shakespearean Tragedy* (1904) is of the first importance for its sense of the tragic idea and offers many new and profound insights into the four major tragedies. G. WILSON KNIGHT'S *The Wheel of Fire* (1930) and *The Imperial Theme* (1931) are largely devoted to Shakespeare's tragedies, and have been rightly among the most influential books in this field, at their most happy when the critic's concern was with the nature of Shakespeare's language and its effect. HARLEY GRANVILLE-BARKER'S *Prefaces to Shakespeare* (1927–54) included comment on *Hamlet, Othello, Lear, Coriolanus* and *Antony and Cleopatra*, from the point of view of a man of the theatre, thus complementing the work of Bradley and Knight. L. C. KNIGHTS manifested a rebellion against Bradley in the title of his *How Many Children had Lady Macbeth?* (Cambridge, 1933; reprinted in *Explorations*, 1946), and in his later writings (notably *Some Shakespearean Themes*, 1957, and *Further Explorations*, 1965) has explored the perennial element in Shakespeare's thought. Studies of particular plays have come from ROBERT B. HEILMAN – *This Great Stage* (Baton Rouge, 1948) on *Lear* and *Magic in the Web* (Lexington, 1956) on *Othello*. L. L. SCHÜCK-ING's *Character Problems in Shakespeare's Plays* (translated 1922), E. E. STOLL's *Art and Artifice in Shakespeare* (1933), J. I. M. STEWART's *Character and Motive in Shakespeare* (1949) have important references to the tragedies – Schücking's stress being on the relation of Shakespeare's work to Elizabethan dramatic practice, Stoll's on the conventional and basically theatrical quality that he found in the plays, Stewart's on the way that modern psychology helps us in a Bradleyan approach to characterization. ERNEST JONES's *Hamlet and Oedipus* (1949) is the major Freudian study of a Shakespearian tragedy. WILLIAM ROSEN in *Shakespeare and the Craft of Tragedy* (Cambridge, Massachusetts, 1960) returns to Bradley, with considerable profit, in his emphasis on the structure of the plays. NICHOLAS BROOKE's *Shakespeare's Early Tragedies* (1968) and JOHN HOLLOWAY's *The Story of the Night: Studies in Shakespeare's Major Tragedies* (1961) also make important contributions to our understanding of Shakespeare's work in the tragic Kind.

Anthologies of critical writings on Shakespeare's tragedies have been edited by ALFRED HARBAGE, *Shakespeare: The Tragedies: A Collection of Critical Essays* (Englewood Cliffs, 1964), by C. LEECH, *Shakespeare: The Tragedies: A Collection of Critical Essays* (Chicago and Toronto, 1965), and by LAURENCE LERNER, *Shakespeare's Tragedies: A Selection of Modern Criticism* (Harmondsworth, 1963).

It is impossible to list here more than a very few of the books on Shakespeare's contemporaries who wrote tragedies. Chiefly notable are: HARRY LEVIN'S *The Overreacher: A Study of Christopher Marlowe* (1954) and J. B. STEANE'S *Marlowe: A Critical Study* (Cambridge, 1964); RUPERT BROOKE'S *John Webster and the Elizabethan Drama* (1917) and GUNNAR BOKLUND'S *The Sources of The White Devil* (Uppsala, Copenhagen, and Cambridge, Massachusetts, 1957) and *The Duchess of Malfi: Sources, Themes, Characters* (Cambridge, Massachusetts, 1962); MILLAR MAC-LURE'S *George Chapman: A Critical Study* (Toronto, 1966); ROBERT DAVRIL'S *Le Drame de John Ford* (Paris, 1954).

Some of the best writing on the tragedies of this time has appeared in the introductions to the New Arden and Revels editions of plays by Shakespeare and his contemporaries.

On the tragedy in general of the Elizabethan–Jacobean years, the following are of special importance: MURIEL BRADBROOK'S *Themes and Conventions of Elizabethan Tragedy* (Cambridge, 1935) and ROBERT ORNSTEIN'S *The Moral Vision of Jacobean Tragedy* (Madison, 1960).

Recent books on Racine include ODETTE DE MOURGUES' *Racine or The Triumph of Relevance* (Cambridge, 1967) and J. C. LAPP'S *Aspects of Racinian Tragedy* (Toronto, 1956).

A standard work on German tragedy is BENNO VON WIESE'S *Die Deutsche Tragödie von Lessing bis Hebbel* (Hamburg, 1948). On Ibsen, the books of MURIEL BRADBROOK, *Ibsen the Norwegian* (1946), and B. W. DOWNS, *Ibsen: The Intellectual Background* (Cambridge, 1946), are particularly to be recommended.

TRAGEDY IN GENERAL

The following collections include extracts from both philosophers and literary critics: LAURENCE MICHEL and RICHARD B.

SEWALL (edd.), *Tragedy: Modern Essays in Criticism* (Englewood Cliffs, 1963); ROBERT W. CORRIGAN (ed.), *Tragedy: Vision and Form* (San Francisco, 1965); NATHAN A. SCOTT, JR. (ed.), *The Tragic Vision and the Christian Faith* (New York, 1957). NIETZSCHE'S *The Birth of Tragedy* can be found conveniently in *The Birth of Tragedy and The Genealogy of Morals*, translated by Francis Golffing (New York, 1956), KIERKEGAARD'S *Fear and Trembling* in *Fear and Trembling and The Sickness unto Death*, translated by Walter Lowrie (New York, 1954). A. C. BRADLEY'S 'Hegel's Theory of Tragedy' (*Oxford Lectures on Poetry*, 1909) is a standard exposition of its subject. MURRAY KRIEGER in *The Tragic Vision* (Chicago and Toronto, 1960), taking his starting-point in Kierkegaard and Nietzsche, argues for a 'formless' tragedy (appropriate, he thinks, to the contemporary situation) which he finds in the novel rather than the drama.

GEORGE STEINER'S *The Death of Tragedy* (1961), T. R. HENN'S *The Harvest of Tragedy* (1956), which deals, after introductory chapters on the nature of the Kind, with tragic and near-tragic writers from Brieux to Lorca, D. D. RAPHAEL'S *The Paradox of Tragedy* (1960), and OSCAR MANDEL'S *A Definition of Tragedy* (New York, 1961) are books on tragedy as a whole that should not be neglected. RICHARD B. SEWALL'S *The Vision of Tragedy* (New Haven, 1959) is a particularly shrewd and balanced study. JEAN JACQUOT'S volume, *Le Théâtre tragique* (Paris, 1962), includes papers given at conferences in France by scholars of international reputation and deals with tragic writing from the ancients to the present day. *Modern Drama: Essays in Criticism*, edited by TRAVIS BOGARD and WILLIAM I. OLIVER (New York, 1965), has a number of essays on tragic or near-tragic writings from Ibsen to Arthur Miller.

Index

Addison, Joseph, 6, 20, 22
Aeschylus, 12–14, 27, 44, 57, 70
Agamemnon, 12, 44, 45, 71, 74
Ajax, 45
Alcestis, 13
All for Love, 5
Ambassadors, The, 7
Anderson, Maxwell, 27
Andromaque, 19
Anna Karenina, 31
Anouilh, Jean, 8–9, 26, 27, 40
Antigone (Anouilh), 8–9, 26, 40
Antigone (Sophocles), 24, 40, 46, 49, 57
Antonio's Revenge, 3–4, 67
Antony and Cleopatra, 36, 45, 57, 73, 83
Arden of Feversham, 35
Aristotle, 1, 2, 14, 17, 18, 28, 30 33,
  37–40, 43–5, 47–9, 56, 58, 61–4, 66,
  67, 70, 72, 74, 82, 83
As You Like It, 68
Atheist's Tragedy, The, 16
Atkins, J. W. H., 2

Bacchae, 40, 42
Back to Methusaleh, 28
Beaumont, Francis, and Fletcher, John,
  16–17, 34
Beckett, Samuel, 76
Beddoes, Thomas Lovell, 25
Before Breakfast, 45
Bérénice, 4–5, 19, 68
Bethell, N., 11

Billy Budd, 31, 37–9, 78
Birthday Party, The, 68, 80
Blakeney, E. H., 71, 78, 83
Blood Wedding, 63
Bogan, L., 6
Bogard, T., 86
Boklund, G., 85
Bond, Edward, 80
Book of Job, The, 78
Bottomley, Gordon, 25
Bradbrook, Muriel, 85
Bradley, A. C., 7–8, 31–2, 38, 57, 73–4,
  83–4, 86
Brand, 21
Brecht, Bertolt, 18, 28, 80
Brieux, Eugène, 86
Brook, Peter, 50
Brooke, N., 24, 84
Brooke, Rupert, 85
Browning, Robert, 25
Büchner, Georg, 21, 63, 65, 81
Bull from the Sea, The, 53, 66
Burlador de Sevilla, El, 19
Butcher, S. H., 33, 47, 48, 82
Byron, George Gordon, Lord, 25
Bywater, I., 1, 37, 61–2, 64, 66, 82

Calderón de la Barca, Pedro, 19, 39
Caligula, 27
Camus, Albert, 27, 31
Caretaker, The, 29, 76, 80
Carpentier, Alejo, 54

Castelvetro, Lodovico, 18, 49, 74
Catiline, 36
Cenci, The, 25
Chapman, George, 4, 16, 19, 40, 65, 67, 85
Chaucer, Geoffrey, 2, 15, 34
Chekhov, Anton, 27, 28, 75, 81
Chemins de la liberté, Les, 68
Chrysippus, 41
Clarissa Harlowe, 30
Cocktail Party, The, 13, 73
Cocteau, Jean, 28, 45
Coleridge, Samuel Taylor, 21, 22, 25
Comedy of Errors, The, 74
Condition humaine, La, 31, 37, 38
Confidential Clerk, The, 13
Conrad, Joseph, 31, 46, 78, 81
Conspiracy and Tragedy of Charles Duke of Byron, The, 65
Coriolanus, 36, 57, 83
Corneille, Pierre, 18, 83
Corrigan, R. W., 23, 86
Creditors, 22
Cymbeline, 16

Dance of Death, The, 22
Danton's Death, 21, 63, 65
Davril, R., 85
Death of a Salesman, 38
Deirdre, 26, 57–8, 72
Deirdre of the Sorrows, 26, 27, 57–8
Diomedes, 2, 15, 34
Doctor Faustus, 16, 34, 63, 64, 71, 73, 79
Dorey, T. A., 83
Downs, B. W., 85
Dream Play, A, 22
Dryden, John, 5, 20, 27
Duchess of Malfi, The, 24, 36, 43, 45, 46, 63, 85
Dudley, D. R., 83

Edward II, 43, 46, 65
Elective Affinities, 6
Eliot, T. S., 13, 25, 27, 31, 58, 73, 75, 83
Ellis-Fermor, Una, 57
Else, G. F., 49
Enemy of the People, An, 22
English Traveller, The, 35
Espoir, L', 31
Etranger, L', 31
Eumenides, 70
Euripides, 12–14, 21, 27, 33, 34, 44, 70
Eurydice, 27
Events while guarding the Bofors Gun, 29, 63, 66, 68, 76, 81

Family Reunion, The, 27, 73
Father, The, 21, 65, 68
Faust, 21
Fielding, Henry, 31
Fille pour du vent, Une, 26
Flaubert, Gustave, 31
Flecker, James Elroy, 65
Fletcher, John. *See under* Beaumont, Francis.
Ford, John, 67, 85
Frazer, Sir James, 53
Freud, Sigmund, 32

Galantière, L., 8–9
Galsworthy, John, 38
Garnier, Robert, 18
Gascoigne, George, 27
Gassner, J., 69
Ghosts, 65
Ghost Sonata, The, 22, 28
Gide, André, 28
Gielgud, Sir John, 50
Gilbert, S., 52
Giraudoux, Jean, 27
Goethe, Johann W. von, 6, 21, 22
Golffing, F., 7, 86

Gorboduc, 16, 70
Granville-Barker, Harley, 83
Greene, W. C., 41, 82
Greville, Fulke, Lord Brooke, 17, 70
Guerre de Troie n'aura pas lieu, La, 27

Hamlet, 20–3, 29, 35, 38, 40, 42, 44, 53,
    57, 59, 63, 64, 73, 74, 78, 79, 82, 83
Harbage, A., 84
Hardy, Thomas, 31, 78
Hassan, 65
Hawthorne, Nathaniel, 31
Hedda Gabler, 21
Hegel, G. W. F., 21–3, 40, 57, 86
Heilman, R. B., 84
Helen, 13
Henn, T. R., 86
Henry V, 58, 70
Henry VI, 35, 57
Henry VIII, 57
Heywood, Thomas, 35
Hill, D. M., 50
Hollander, R., 77
Holloway, J., 51, 84
Homer, 63
Hopkins, John, 10, 55
Horace, 18, 49, 71, 78, 83
House, H., 48, 62–3, 82
House of Bernarda Alba, The, 74
Huis Clos, 75

Ibsen, Henrik, 18, 21, 22, 27, 28, 65,
    75–6, 81, 85–6
Iliad, The, 30
Ion, 13
Iphigenia in Tauris, 13, 62
Isidore of Seville, 2, 15, 34
I Thought of Daisy, 66

Jacquot, J., 86
James, Henry, 7, 31, 69

Jameson, Anna, 59
Jaspers, Karl, 23
Jocasta, 27
John of Garland, 2
John Gabriel Borkman, 21
Jones, Edmund D., 3
Jones, Ernest, 84
Jones, John, 82
Jonson, Ben, 19, 28, 36
Jude the Obscure, 31, 78
Julius Caesar, 45, 46
Juno and the Paycock, 37, 40
Justice, 38

Kermode, F., 25
Kierkegaard, Søren, 6, 21–3, 86
King Lear, 16, 20, 24, 36, 38, 40, 49–
    51, 53, 57, 59, 63, 66, 74, 83–4
King must Die, The, 53
Kinwelmersh, Francis, 27
Kitto, H. D. F., 41, 45, 82
Kleist, Heinrich von, 6, 21, 81
Knight from Olmeda, The, 19
Knight, G. Wilson, 83–4
Knights, L. C., 84
Krieger, M., 78, 86

Lady from the Sea, The, 22
Lapp, J. C., 85
Lee, Nathaniel, 27
Lerner, L., 84
Lessing, Gotthold Ephraim, 48
Levin, H., 85
Little Eyolf, 22
Lloyd-Evans, G., 83
Lock, W., 61, 63
Lope de Vega Carpio, 19
Lorca, Federico García, 29, 63, 74, 86
Lord Jim, 31, 46
Lost Steps, The, 54–5
Love's Labour's Lost, 74

Lowrie, W., 6, 86
Lowry, Malcolm, 31
Lucas, D. W., 63, 82
Lucas, F. L., 49–50, 56, 62–3, 82, 83
Lust's Dominion, or The Lascivious Queen, 3, 77
Lynceus, 61–2

Macbeth, 34, 36, 40, 42, 43, 57, 63, 64, 74, 84
McGrath, John, 29, 63, 76, 80
Machine infernale, La, 28
MacLure, M., 85
MacNeice, Louis, 71
Madame Bovary, 31
Maid's Tragedy, The, 16–17
Malraux, André, 31, 37, 77
Mandel, O., 86
Margeson, J. M. R., 83
Maria Stuart, 21
Marlowe, Christopher, 16, 18, 34, 43, 44, 46, 65, 71, 79, 85
Marovitz, Charles, 50
Marston, John, 3–4, 67
Mask of Apollo, The, 14
Maxwell, J. C., 23
Mayer, E., 6
Mayor of Zalamea, The, 19, 39
Medea (Anouilh), 26
Medea (Euripides), 42, 49
Melville, Herman, 31, 37, 39, 78
Merry Wives of Windsor, The, 75
Michel, L., 23, 85–6
Middleton, Thomas, 67, 80
Miller, Arthur, 38, 43, 63, 74, 86
Milton, John, 17, 47–8, 49
Miss Julie, 21, 63
Moby Dick, 31, 78
Moncrieff, C. K. Scott, 24
Monk's Tale, The, 2
Mother Courage and her Children, 80

Mouches, Les, 26, 27, 51–3
Mourgues, Odette de, 85
Mourning Becomes Electra, 26, 27, 72–3
Mrozek, Slavomir, 11
Murder in the Cathedral, 71–3
Mustapha, 17, 70

Nicoll, A., 12, 82
Nietzsche, Friedrich, 7, 21, 22, 86
Norton, Thomas, 16, 70
Nostromo, 31, 46, 78, 81

Obey, André, 26
O'Casey, Sean, 26, 37, 40
Odyssey, The, 30
Oedipus (Dryden and Lee), 27
Oedipus (Gide), 28
Oedipus (Sophocles), 41, 44, 45, 49, 51, 53, 61, 66, 71
Oliver, W. I., 86
Olson, E., 69, 82–3
O'Neill, Eugene, 26, 27, 45, 72
Onés, Harriet de, 55
Oresteia, 13, 14, 24, 26, 27, 40, 45, 57, 72, 82
Ornstein, R. H., 85
Othello, 34, 38, 40–2, 55, 59, 63, 74, 83–4
Ovid, 79

Painter of Dishonour, The, 19
Peer Gynt, 21, 22
Penthesilea, 6, 21
Peste, La, 31
Phèdre, 19, 20, 24, 72
Phillips, Stephen, 25
Phoenissae, 27
Phoenix and Turtle, The, 4
Pinero, Sir Arthur Wing, 73
Pinter, Harold, 29, 68, 76, 80, 81

Plato, 30, 47
Plough and the Stars, The, 37
Point of Departure, 27
Prince of Homburg, The, 21
Prometheia, 13, 14
Prometheus Bound, 13
Proust, Marcel, 24, 59
Puttenham, George, 3

Racine, Jean, 4–5, 18–20, 32, 68, 72, 85
Raphael, D. D., 18–19, 86
Red Roses for Me, 37
Renault, Mary, 14, 53, 66
Revenge of Bussy D'Ambois, The, 4
Richard II, 42, 57
Richard III, 38, 43
Richards, I. A., 8, 56–7
Richardson, Samuel, 30, 31, 35
Riders to the Sea, 26
Romeo and Juliet, 39, 45, 70, 73
Rosen, W., 84
Rosencrantz and Guildenstern are Dead, 10, 29, 36–7, 63, 65, 77
Rouge et le Noir, Le, 31
Royal Hunt of the Sun, The, 80
Russell, Bertrand, 10, 55
Rymer, Thomas, 5, 20, 38, 42

Sackville, Thomas, 16, 70
Samson Agonistes, 17, 47–9
Sanders, W., 42, 79
Sartre, Jean-Paul, 26, 51–3, 68, 75
Saved, 80
Scaliger, J. C., 74
Scarlet Letter, The, 31
Schiller, J. C. F. von, 21
Schücking, L. L., 84
Scott, Nathan A., Jr., 39, 86
Second Mrs Tanqueray, The, 73
Sejanus, 36

Seneca, 15–18, 34, 70, 83
Sewall, R. B., 23, 85–6
Shadow of a Gunman, The, 37
Shadowy Waters, The, 72
Shaffer, Peter, 80
Shakespeare, William, 4, 16, 18, 20, 25, 27–8, 32, 34, 36, 39, 42, 44, 45, 51, 56, 59, 62, 67, 72, 74, 80, 83–5
Shaw, George Bernard, 28
Shelley, Percy Bysshe, 25
Sidney, Sir Philip, 2–3, 16, 33, 34, 40
Silver Tassie, The, 37
Sophocles, 12–14, 27, 32, 33, 44, 45, 53, 70, 82
Steane, J. B., 85
Steegman, A., 83
Steiner, G., 9, 80, 86
Stendhal, 31
Stewart, J. I. M., 84
Stewart, R., 39
Stoll, E. E., 84
Stoppard, Tom, 10, 11, 29, 32, 63, 65, 77, 80
Strindberg, August, 21, 22, 27–9, 45, 63, 65, 68, 75–6, 81
Stronger, The, 45
Swann's Way, 59
Swinburne, Algernon Charles, 25, 28
Synge, John Millington, 26, 27, 57–8

Talking to a Stranger, 10
Tamburlaine, 16, 34, 36, 44, 63, 64
Tango, 11
Tempest, The, 74
Temptation of the West, The, 77
Tennyson, Alfred Lord, 25
Tess of the D'Urbervilles, 31, 78
Theobald, Lewis, 20
Theodectes, 61
Three Sisters, The, 29
Tiger at the Gates, 27

Tirso de Molina, 19
Tolstoy, Count Leo, 31
Tourneur, Cyril, 16, 80
Trevelyan, H., 6
Troilus and Cressida, 16
Trojan Women, The, 13, 14, 45, 46, 55, 64, 65, 67, 68
Twelfth Night, 68

Unamuno, Miguel de, 23
Uncle Vanya, 29
Under the Volcano, 31, 78, 81

Vahlen, Johannes, 61–4
Vailland, Roger, 75
Vida, Marco Girolamo, 18
View from the Bridge, A, 43, 63, 74
Voix humaine, La, 45

Waiting for Godot, 76
Walker, A., 3
Watling, E. F., 71
Webster, John, 36, 43, 45, 46, 67, 80, 85
Wedekind, Frank, 28
White Devil, The, 36, 46, 85
Wiese, Benno von, 85
Wild Duck, The, 21
Wiles, P., 75
Willcock, G. D., 3
Wilson, Edmund, 66
Within a Budding Grove, 24
Woman Killed with Kindness, A, 35
Wordsworth, William, 25
Wozzeck, 21

Yeats, W. B., 26, 27, 57–8, 72
Young Trout, A, 75